EUCHARIST
AT THE CENTER
CONTINUALLY FORMING THE PARISH

Eucharist at the Center
Copyright © 2019 by Fr. Art Baranowski and Theresa Doyle.
All rights reserved.

No part of this book may be used or reproduced in any manner whatsoever without written permission, except in the case of brief quotations embodied in critical articles and reviews. For more information, e-mail all inquiries to info@mindstirmedia.com.

Published by Mindstir Media, LLC
45 Lafayette Rd | Suite 181| North Hampton, NH 03862 | USA
1.800.767.0531 | www.mindstirmedia.com

Printed in the United States of America
ISBN-13: 978-1-7342210-2-2
Library of Congress Control Number: 2019917517

Over the many years of his faithful priestly ministry, Fr. Baranowski has shown himself to be an effective pastor, whose ability to flourish in a variety of different parish contexts attests to his steadiness and leadership. He is known to be a balanced pastor whose efforts have borne fruit in the lives of parishioners through his ability not only to lead parishioners in developing their own relationship with God, but also in guiding them to strengthen their relationship with their parish community.

—The Most Reverend Allen H. Vigneron
Archbishop of Detroit

Theresa Doyle is an inspirational Catholic leader with a clarity of vision for parish life and ministry. In my interaction with her over many years about Small Church Communities, she has greatly impressed me with her facility in helping folks to make their parish more fully what God desires it to be. Her communication skills and humble but confident personality enable her effectiveness in helping people find the path to holiness in and through parish community.

—Fr. Charles F. Klinger, Ph.D Pastor,
St. Paul the Apostle Parish, Westerville, Ohio

<u>Eucharist at the Center</u> *caps decades of Fr. Art and Theresa promoting a small church community vision for parish by focusing on the heart of the matter; the Church responding and celebrating Jesus Lord of communities of missionary disciples.*

—Bro. Robert Moriarty, S.M. Director of the Pastoral Department
for Small Christian Communities
(Archdiocese of Hartford) 1989-2017

EUCHARIST
AT THE CENTER
CONTINUALLY FORMING THE PARISH

Fr Art Baranowski & Theresa Doyle

OVERVIEW OF THE BOOK:
EUCHARIST AT THE CENTER
CONTINUALLY FORMING THE PARISH

For the Catholic Church to rediscover its life and energy, the Church will have to pay attention to the parish itself. The one lasting source of parish renewal is the same as it always has been: the Eucharist. It is the main way Christ forms his Church. It is our Source and Summit. But for the Eucharist to form parishioners deeply, they have to come prepared and attentive. Many Catholics come to Mass severely limited in their ability to hear and to respond. They live in a culture that continually forms them to be "on the go," overly stimulated, and lacking in silence and depth. This book focuses entirely on preparing the minds and hearts of parishioners for the upcoming Sunday Eucharist in ways that are simple enough for anyone to do. The pastor and pastoral leaders need to keep focused on this one goal and not let the many distractions that take so much time and energy get in the way. Implementing this vision will take some time and energy, but pastors and those doing the work with him will find great energy in the fruits. This book is a practical and realistic approach to staying about the basic purpose of the parish. Letting the Eucharist be what it is truly meant to be is the only thing that will transform parish.

> "The Church evangelizes and is herself evangelized through the beauty of the liturgy which is both a celebration and the source of her renewed self-giving."
>
> Pope Francis *The Joy of the Gospel*

TABLE OF CONTENTS

Foreword 1

What a pastor of 25 years finds attractive and necessary for the parish presented in this book. by Fr. Bill Thaden Lorain, Ohio

What This Book is About.. 5

This book is about Parish and creating a Parish where everything is centered on the main way Christ forms his Church.

Chapter 1: How We Do Mass.. 9

It is not simply what we do but who we are. From the Mass we are sent.

**Chapter 2: The Sunday Eucharist:
Can We Hold On To Our Young People?**................................... 13

It is possible! Young people will need to see an adult Church where people connect everyday life to the Liturgy.

Chapter 3: Keeping the Liturgy Focused..................................... 19

Many Catholics have not met Jesus Christ through the Church. Let Christ do what he intends to do in and through the Liturgy.

**Chapter 4: Sunday Eucharist's Challenge –
The Way Parishioners are Living Today** 29

What the Eucharist is meant to be contrasted with the way many parishioners come to Mass. – The challenge due to the unprecedented changes in today's culture.

Chapter 5: The Parish Sunday Eucharist...................................... 35

The overriding goal of the Parish – Getting parishioners to the Eucharist prepared to hear and be transformed.

Chapter 6: The Parish Structured for the Eucharist 41

Deliberately focusing everything in the parish to form people for the next Eucharist. The two necessary structures are: 1. doing the existing programs differently (coloring the parish) and 2. the formation of small church communities

Chapter 7: Small Church Communities.. 53

Small Church Communities as a counter structure so the Word of God finds a better soil to penetrate and grow.

Chapter 8: Building the Parish from the Ground Up 59

The primary tool of evangelization is the experience of the community, people and priest, at the Sunday Eucharist. Putting our effort toward building that community.

Chapter 9: The Pastor of the Parish.. 65

The absolute need for the pastor to stay centered on the basic purpose of the parish. The pastor begins with a deeper hearing of the Sunday gospel as well as hearing the gospel in the communal setting of a small group.

Chapter 10: Beginnings 75

Practical steps any one can do. Conclusion – every pastor will decide the focus of the parish and where he will put his energy

Appendices 89

Appendix 1 – Initiating and Forming
a New Small Church Community 89

Directives and agendas for first 8 meetings

Appendix 2 – Agenda for the Maturing
and the Mature Small Church Community............................... 101

Appendix 3 – Prayer Cards... 105

FOREWORD

Father William Thaden
Pastor, Sacred Heart Chapel (Parish) Lorain, Ohio

I once heard the Carmelite priest, hermit and wild man, William McNamara, say, "Don't read good books. There is not enough time for that. Read only the great ones." That has always stuck with me, not so much in forming a reading list, but for the sense that we have precious little time and it is important that we use it only for the most important things.

It was within my first three years of priesthood that I began to question the effectiveness of all of our many efforts in the parish. We worked hard. There were the requisite councils, pastoral and finance, along with several commissions and a parish school. We sought to preach and worship well, to prepare our young people and inquirers for the sacraments, to minister to the sick and dying and to serve the poor. We made efforts to evangelize, going door-to-door in the neighborhood and inviting folks. But at the end of the day, I often didn't see the rich fruit of lives converted to Christ. Ignorance of the most fundamental elements of our Catholic faith was the norm. Young adults were largely absent and it seemed that the non-denominational churches kept picking off our people one by one, who would then explain that "over there" they found Christ, began to learn the Scriptures and felt welcomed into a real community of faith.

I am over twenty-five years ordained now, in the Diocese of Cleveland, and have served as pastor here for the past fourteen years. I love being a parish priest and hope to serve in parish ministry until the Lord calls me home. But if I am going to offer my life this way, then I need to feel that I'm giving myself for the most important things, for a ministry that will truly lead to where Christ is calling us as a Church and specifically as parishes. Over these years I have found inspiration and practical direction in Father Art Baranowski and Theresa Doyle. Art's first book, *Creating Small Church Communities*, seemed to ask the right questions and expressed the same dissatisfaction with the status quo in parishes that I was feeling but didn't know what to do with. Sharing his experience, he offered a concrete plan for a different model of parish, one based on a return to silence, reflection and the sharing of our faith in community.

As pastor I have gradually attempted to implement that vision, to restructure the parish, to change the way we operate. We are continually attempting to make every contact people have with the parish an experience of Church in the best sense, an experience with the living Christ. I am working closely with the pastoral facilitators of our small church communities, offering ongoing formation and support. The fruits are indisputable. Those who have engaged in this process have found themselves on a journey to a deeper experience of faith and specifically of being Church. Each one has his or her own testimony.

When I dedicate my time for this work I am constantly reaffirmed that I am not wasting my time or life energy. I am grateful to be able to benefit from Art's many years of experience in this work.

This new book has a focus and grounding not found in the first. As a Catholic and as a priest I am excited by Father Art's and Theresa Doyle's laser-like focus on the priority of the Sunday Eucharist. The small church community is not the goal in this model of parish. It is the structure that, I would join in arguing, best leads us into a transformative participation in the Sunday Mass. Again, Father Art and Theresa give expression to what in my experience resonates as true. Nowhere else have I seen an approach to small communities or, for that matter, to parish, that draws so deeply, faithfully and practically on the best of our Catholic faith tradition. I believe this work will offer new hope and clarity to pastors and parishioners all over who are pouring their lives out for the Church but longing to see a more profound awakening to a lived faith. Albert Einstein famously said that it is insanity to keep doing the same thing but expect a different result. If you still have fire in your belly for the mission of Christ in and through the Church, if you are willing to rock the boat for the best reasons, then this book is for you.

WHAT THIS BOOK IS ABOUT

This book is about giving hope to any parish by focusing on the one and only activity that ultimately can transform its people—the Sunday Eucharist. This entire book is written to address two questions:

- How can the Mass have a greater influence on the lives of parishioners?
- How can the Sunday Eucharist become a more transforming experience for the parish community itself?

The parish is where the faith is practiced and learned for the vast majority of Catholics. The parish is the experienced community of faith. If there is to be a vibrant Catholic Church, that Church will happen in the parish and not in particular movements—at least, in North America at this time. The parish is where the Gospel is heard or not heard, where people are transformed or not.

No matter the size of any parish, its income, or the particular gifts of the pastor: the one central life-giving experience of each parish is the celebration of the Eucharist. Yet, so many Catholics lack understanding of that celebration and, more importantly, how to enter in.

Eucharist at the Center Volume 1 is about what the Church says the Sunday Eucharist is meant to be. It focuses on helping parishioners come to the liturgy prepared to hear and to listen, since how we come to Mass greatly influences the degree to which we are able to deeply hear the voice of Christ in his Word. People's transformation is more limited when they do not have a personal engagement with his words. So, this first volume is about the parish preparing its people during the week for the upcoming Sunday.

We will present details for two simple and clear structures to help parishioners come to Mass better prepared for deeper listening.

1. With existing programs, activities, and committees (what already is happening in the parish), there is introduced a short time with the upcoming Sunday gospel. People simply listen to the gospel, spend a little silence with it, reflect on a few life-connection questions, and speak to one or two others.
2. The parish gradually begins a new structure of small church communities led by trained lay leaders who work under the direction of the pastor and staff. These communities of 8-12 adults meet regularly to focus on the next Sunday's gospel.

We believe that people must be given a way, in addition to the homily, to help each other hear the gospel. We (the authors) know from experience that ordinary Catholics can impact each other's faith deeply as they help each other prepare for the Eucharist. But pastors and other parish leaders will need to make parishioner sharing on the gospel a priority so the entire parish will be enlivened over time. We realize that pastors and their associates will not be convinced simply by reading this book. Therefore, this book offers one simple recommendation that a pastor experiences for several months a small group of very ordinary parishioners sharing on the upcoming Sunday gospel. Once a pastor can see and experience for himself what happens when a small group of regular parishioners engages with the gospel, then he can decide whether he wants to commit the parish to this direction.

Why would any pastor make the choice to form the parish in the disciplined way we are describing unless he personally knows the benefit coming back to the parish?

WHAT EUCHARIST AT THE CENTER VOLUME 2 IS ABOUT

- Recall the vision.
- The small church community: its format and its process.
- Beginning a few small groups with one very basic training session for their leaders.
- Further training of small group leaders (18 hours) and 1st leader retreat including the format and outlines for the leaders' formation.
- Conversion Experience, for example, Alpha, ChristLife or Christ Renews His Parish especially targeting younger married and single parishioners. How to transition into small church communities.
- Formation of the parish staff in the Vision and its implementation as they function in their individual ministries.
- Homilies
- Suggestions for a more effective Sunday Eucharist.

This model is structured around lay pastoral leaders in charge of small communities throughout the parish. It means the pastor has a group of trained leaders working with him and sharing a common vision with him. Catholic pastors, often overwhelmed and overextended, have found a tremendous support in working with these leaders.

What our book describes actually is happening.

It is both **traditional** and **innovative**. Traditional because it builds the parish around the Eucharist and because the pastor and his leadership are key for this to happen. Traditional also since the Church always has taught that the faith awareness the people bring to Mass is vital. Innovative because the goal is for as many parishioners as possible to help each other to genuinely hear the gospel as the Church hears the gospel. Innovative because of new structures like small communities and an entirely new group of focused lay leaders working with the pastor toward this vision of parish.

Chapter One
HOW WE DO MASS

For I received from the Lord what I also handed on to you, that the Lord Jesus, on the night he was handed over, took bread, and, after he had given thanks, broke it and said, "This is my body that is for you. Do this in remembrance of me."
1 Corinthians 11, 23-24

By Father Art

I came as the new pastor to St. Christopher Parish in Marysville, Michigan on Christmas Eve 1996. I had been pastor of several suburban parishes and had been the founding pastor of a new parish where I stayed for over ten years.

From that experience I spent the next five years doing national and international work. I had met with priests and pastoral leaders in most of the U.S. dioceses, many dioceses of Canada, Australia, and elsewhere. These pastors and their staffs were looking for a way that parishioners could hear more deeply the Scriptures proclaimed on Sunday and to see in those Scriptures a way to look at their everyday lives. Meeting in small communities led by trained facilitators was one indispensable means for this goal to happen.

When I came to St. Christopher, I was ordained for twenty-eight years. Since my beginning as a priest, I was convinced that the ordinary parishioners needed to hear each other's faith if a parish was to be spiritually alive. Some sharing groups I experienced in the seminary and a visionary priest in the Lansing Diocese helped me see this. But, how could people hear each other's faith? By and large, parishes were not structured so the average parishioners ever heard each other speak of the gospel of Sunday and make connections to everyday life. Most of the regular and irregular parishioners had never done this.

I spent my first twenty-eight years as a priest finding ways that common ordinary people could help each other listen to the Sunday gospel. With mistakes and missteps along the way, I and others plodded in this single direction of finding ways that worked. What I knew for sure was that the majority of parishioners, who saw themselves as nothing special and did not see themselves as the "religious" types, had to experience themselves as belonging at the Sunday liturgy.

So, there I was for the very first time at St. Christopher. It was the Christmas Eve, mid-night Mass. Behind and to the left of the altar was the choir in flowing robes and on risers about the same level as the ambo/altar platform. The musical group dominated the singing. At Communion, one of the robed members (also a communion minister) came forward to take the Eucharist to the choir. At the announcement time, the president of the parish council, also a choir member, came forward to the microphone to welcome me to the parish. All the people clapped. I thanked everyone but I was deeply troubled.

To me, that first Mass with St. Christopher Parish seemed to put the people into the mode of an audience. Perhaps they were moved and uplifted by the choir, but still an audience. At one particularly beautiful piece by the music group, the people clapped in appreciation. That is what an audience does.

Where was my discomfort at that liturgy coming from, I had to ask myself? My own narrow opinion about how Sunday Mass should look? A lack of respect for the way this particular parish chooses to celebrate? No appreciation for diversity? My life's work as a priest had been what I thought the Church wanted: making the parishioners assembled around Christ at the altar the central focus. Was I wrong to keep insisting on that focus?

My problem at that liturgy was not shared by anyone else in the parish. People simply were used to being inspired by the talented musicians. The music group included some of the most involved members of the parish and the choir members were dedicated parishioners who gave many hours of their time to the practices. They really cared and wanted to serve the parish.

In the years' following that Christmas Eve liturgy, the one question that needed to be asked continually was this: Where is our focus meant to be at Mass? It took many meetings over several years and some help from the archdiocese to critique our parish liturgies. Slowly the focus began to shift.

We came to see that our attention at the Eucharist celebrations certainly had to be on Jesus Christ as the central agent. He is the one who makes things happen. And, Christ is acting to form his body and the people are that body. Christ's own focus is on his people. So, our focus at the liturgies slowly began to shift more toward the people at Mass. We deliberately treated the people as Church. These two volumes speak to what treating people as Church means, especially in the celebration of the Eucharist.

I remained at that parish as its pastor for my last twenty years in active ministry. Over those twenty years, Theresa Doyle, the co-author of this book, was my closest collaborator. She and I worked together for that entire time. Theresa and her husband Chris brought a deep commitment to the Church and we shared the vision for parish presented in this book. Theresa Doyle worked primarily with the lay leaders of the small communities which prepared parishioners to come to the Sunday Eucharist more disposed for transformation. She knows what it takes to move a parish into this new direction.

Take time to talk to someone about the questions at the end of each chapter.

What attracts you in this opening chapter?

Where do you find questions, disagreements or resistance?
Try to put those into a few sentences.

Chapter Two

THE SUNDAY EUCHARIST:

CAN WE HOLD ON TO OUR YOUNG PEOPLE!

*My son, you are here with me always;
everything I have is yours.*

Luke 15:31

By Theresa Doyle

My husband Chris and I were both raised in strong Catholic families. We honestly thought that our children would share in our love for the Church. However, our four children began meeting more and more friends with no connection to the Church. The Church as the center for our lives became less and less attractive to our children. Their friends came from families getting along quite well without the need for faith or a faith community.

Along with that, our pastor continually was preaching about "love and community", a strong emphasis in the 80's. The glaring reality was the parish felt little like a community. People came and went from Mass but connected little to each other. There were some connections in the parish but generally they served people of similar interests.

What was becoming apparent to me was that our children, who were in Catholic school, were experiencing a great disconnect between what they were taught and what they experienced: not only in the school environment but in the parish at large. One of the glaring statements that spoke of this disconnect was when my fourteen-year-old daughter said after Mass one day, "Mom, nobody really cares if we are here or not." Another statement was, "I really think that you and dad are the only ones who believe this stuff." Doubtless these were reactions from teenagers going through a questioning and testing stage. But, comments like this continued throughout the years, even into adulthood. Chris and I persistently tried to help our children live as Catholics and above all to appreciate the Mass.

Another telling statement was made by my son when he was in 9th grade in our Catholic high school. Quite taken by the obvious faith of his religion teacher he said to me, "This is the first teacher I have had that I think really believes this." Did his other teachers have faith? No doubt most did. I believe the issue is that a great number of Catholics, including teachers, make many things seem important and often don't even speak of their own personal faith. Faith and being part of the Church can appear to be incidental.

My husband and I prayed intently for our children. At the same time more and more people were leaving the Church altogether or coming to Mass only occasionally. It was becoming clearer to me that parishes had to be different in some way. In the midst of this frustration, I was approached by our pastor to consider studying youth ministry in our diocese. It meant four years of studying and then accepting a position in the parish. It seemed clear to Chris and me that God was calling me to this work. How could we be praying so hard for young people in the Church and not consider some action to help their faith?

If youth ministry is considered successful because one gathers a large number of kids every week for an evening or afternoon to have a great time with all the right elements of prayer, experiential catechesis, friends, food and lots of adult faith role models - then I was among the most successful Coordinators of Youth Ministry. But in reality, I knew there was nothing successful in all the efforts of gathering young people in a parish, or in a Catholic school for that matter, if you cannot get them to Mass and appreciate Mass on Sunday.

I am not advocating that Mass simply be entertaining. Many parishes have tried that route i.e. more contemporary music, bell choirs, etc. What I became convinced of is that young people need to see adults believing that they are the Church at the Sunday celebration and in everyday life. How we look—our attention, our reverence, our connections to each other around Christ present—speaks to our young people. How we are together is the message. When the adults are not "into it" at Mass, why would our young people be drawn in and find a reason to come back.

I don't mean only singing all the responses and hymns. Though that surely is important, there is much more needed. It is necessary that our young people, as well as everyone at Mass, experience a community engaged spiritually and humanly with Christ speaking his word right here and right now. And, experience people consciously connected to each other as the Body of Christ. By witnessing what it means to be a Eucharistic people together at Mass, people learn to be a Eucharistic people in their lives during the rest of the week. The way this kind of community can happen is why Father Art and I are writing this book.

After seven years of working hard in youth ministry, I began to see that working with youth was simply not making a difference in the parish at large and the parish was not really making a difference in the lives of the youth. Like many parishes, we were pretty good at doing things but we didn't experience being Church very well.

In 1997, I came to work at St. Christopher Parish because of the way Father Art was deliberately structuring the parish into small communities. The purpose was to get parishioners to hear the upcoming gospel as a way to look at their ordinary lives and decisions. It simply made sense because the vision was not about a particular program but about forming the parish community itself. This vision is not anything new. In fact, it is more about going back to the early Church when people simply helped each other be Church and experience the living God forming his people through his Word and Eucharist.

My work at St. Christopher has been about creating structures, including small church communities, so the people of the parish help each other gather around the Word and enter more fully into the Eucharistic prayer; that great exchange of Christ with his people. The result is people of the parish not only regularly evangelizing each other but giving each other more confidence to take their faith beyond the parish, to their neighborhoods and work places.

In 2004, I assumed the role of pastoral associate at St. Christopher Parish. Since then I do not work as directly with youth as I once did.

But I see that deliberately working to create a structure in the parish where the youth see and hear the faith of the adult Church and also are given many opportunities to speak of their everyday life and faith has resulted in a viable and vibrant youth ministry. Youth ministry has been fruitful here because it is built on a solid base of a visible adult faith community. The long and the short of it is St. Christopher's became a parish that gathers well as a community of faith because so many people are deliberate about helping each other do so.

Many people who visit St. Christopher Parish comment that there is something different here. These visitors include my now adult children who are married and raising children of their own, living in cities away from their home town. Their current perception of the Church is not much different than what they experienced growing up, except when they come to St. Christopher Parish, they know there is something very different here. The people are different.

It is not that the people of St. Christopher have more faith than any other parish. Nor is Christ any more present in this parish than in any other. It is because there are deliberate structures that bring people to speak and hear the faith of each other and help each other focus on the Sunday Eucharist as central to their lives and central to the parish's life. My contribution to this book is to speak to what we have seen and continue to see.

A FEW OF OUR YOUTH EXPERIENCES

For many people today it is difficult to find godparents and confirmation sponsors from family members or friends who are actively practicing Catholics. What we found happening more and more at St. Christopher's was that parishioners were easily finding them in their own small church community. One example: I once asked an 8th grade boy preparing for Confirmation how he found his sponsor. His response to me was, "Oh he is in our small church community." Though he did not actually attend the small church meeting with his parents, he had gotten to know the people who came to his home to meet and he identified with them.

Another example from a young father:

> "When our daughter was baptized four years ago we had a difficult time finding godparents. Now because we have come to personally know people of faith in the parish, we have many to choose from for our son."

Testimony from a mother and grandmother:

> My husband and I have raised our children and we are raising our grandchildren. For many years we have been part of a small church community. The gospel sharing and preparing for Mass became so ingrained in our family that it was as normal for us as going to school. These are the long-term effects I am seeing on our children and grandchildren.

- *There are many children in our small church community (SCC). During the meeting they play together in the basement, joining us for the closing prayer and refreshments. My eight year old granddaughter asked me if the children could do what the adults were doing and share the gospel of Sunday with each other.*

- *When my two little grandsons were at Mass they would ask when they could go to Communion and when could they meet with people to talk about God.*

- *When our children and grandchildren celebrated 1st Reconciliation, 1st Communion and Confirmation, they looked forward to having our SCC celebrate with them. They were also excited to celebrate when the other children of our group made their sacraments.*

- *Our fifteen-year old son, on arriving home from football practice, made a point to take a few minutes to speak to each and every adult in the SCC who had come to meet at our home. These were parishioners who had become significant to him.*

- *Our grandson grew up with a SCC meeting at our home. At age nineteen he asked me when he could join a SCC.*

- *For us the small church community formed a bridge between our daily family life and the larger Church.*

· ·

Father Art and I are proposing a model that affects everything happening in the parish, a model we both have experienced. This model transforms the parish. We do NOT advocate taking the existing parish and simply adding a few small groups to it. To give this "new" direction to parish, pastors and their staffs will need to keep the parish focused in a very particular way. And because the Eucharist is the heart of the Church, the model we propose forms the parishioners for and through the Eucharist to become disciples.

> If there is youth ministry going on in your parish, does it help youth enter more fully into the Sunday Mass?
>
> Do the young people experience adults, besides their parents, who share their faith with other adults?
>
> Do you have children or grandchildren no longer connected to the Church? What might have helped them stay connected or to return?

Chapter Three
KEEPING THE LITURGY FOCUSED

...for without me, you can do nothing.
John 15:5

You are strangers and aliens no longer. No, you are fellow citizens of the saints and members of the household of God ...in Christ Jesus you are being built into this temple, to become a dwelling place for God in the Spirit.
Ephesians 2:19, 22

This entire book rests on three main foundations given to us by the Church herself. These three teachings are the bedrock not only for the Sunday Eucharist but for everything happening in the parish. In each and every liturgy, they are the fundamentals to focus upon.

1. **The Eucharist is "the source and summit of the Christian life."** The other sacraments, and indeed all ecclesiastical ministries and works of the apostolate, are bound up with the Eucharist, are oriented toward it and flow from it. For in the blessed Eucharist is contained the whole spiritual good of the Church, namely Christ himself, our Pasch.
Catechism of the Catholic Church (CCC) # 1324 quoting Vatican II Constitution on the Church #10

Vatican II calls the Eucharist the **"font and apex of the whole Christian life."** Every other activity in the parish and in our individual and social lives flows from and flows toward the Sunday Eucharist. This awesome celebration has to be as clearly focused as possible.

2. **At the head of the Eucharistic assembly is Christ himself, the principal agent of the Eucharist. It is he who presides invisibly over every Eucharistic celebration.**
CCC # 1348

Jesus as the agent of the Eucharist is said over and over again in the *Catechism*, the *General Instruction on the Roman Missal*, and the *Constitution on the Sacred Liturgy*.

About a year ago as the entrance procession was about to begin, one lector said to me "Showtime!" This may be somewhat crass but it belies a common attitude about the Mass as a thing. In fact, the Sunday Eucharist is an *action* of Jesus Christ, the principal agent. An agent acts and so it is Christ doing the Mass, making happen what only he can make happen. Most traditional Catholics would recognize Christ present under the form of the bread and the wine and; that presence is his most special and unique presence. But he is present throughout the Mass. Christ himself speaks and acts in and through liturgical ministers, the assembly, and the action of the priest. It is Christ, the principal agent acting in each movement:

- Gathering his people, drawing each person
- Speaking his Word so he can prepare his people for communion
- His is the Great Thanksgiving (Eucharistic Prayer) which always ends with "Through Christ, with him, and in him."
- Bringing about communion with himself and so with each other
- Sending his people into the world to carry his communion.
- Every parish probably would acknowledge this presence of Christ. Yet, it can easily be a truth acknowledged but, in the background, not making a practical difference in the Sunday celebration itself. It seems to us that parish celebrations of Mass

are not always sharply focused on Jesus Christ and what he is saying and doing for his people.

So, the focus also is on the People of God. It is Christ's action and the action of his People.

3. **The celebration of the Mass, as the action of Christ and of the People of God arrayed hierarchically, is the center of the whole of Christian life for the Church both universal and local, as well as for each of the faithful individually.**
General Instruction of the Roman Missal (GIRM) # 16

From this it follows that every liturgical celebration, because it is an action of Christ the priest and of His Body the Church, is a sacred action surpassing all others.
Vatican II Constitution on the Sacred Liturgy #7

These three foundational statements are eminently clear about where our attention is to be placed and centered. The Sunday Eucharist is about the interplay of Christ and his People back and forth. Mass is not something we come to but a personal and intimate action and response.

People have to come to the Sunday Eucharist personally more prepared to hear and to be moved for the liturgy to do its work most effectively. All the remaining chapters are centered on the parish helping parishioners come more prepared. However, parishioners will be much less motivated to prepare either individually or in a small community if the Sunday celebration does not seem to support their efforts.

The way we do liturgy can dampen or can help the interior dispositions of people. This chapter looks at the ways people are considered or not considered in the celebration of Sunday Eucharist. Our point is that the people themselves are essential to the celebration.

Some practices in parish Sunday celebrations actually can take the focus away from the true center of the liturgy. We intend to clarify this model for parish by showing what is not helpful. We do not mean to be fault-finding toward what parishes are doing on Sunday nor do we think we know more than everyone else. However, in the parish model we wish to present, there are certain practices and ways of doing things that work best.

What are specific practices and ways of doing weekend worship that help people to have confidence that they really are Church, the Body of Christ? What parish practices can hinder that confidence? What can help parishioners pay attention to the Person of Christ at the center?

Fr. Art

For the last three years, since I turned seventy-three, I have been a senior priest. I no longer direct one particular parish but I have helped at about twenty different parishes, 10% of the parishes of our archdiocese. In three years of retirement, I have had much more exposure to different parishes than in the past twenty years at St. Christopher's. There are three parishes where I am a "regular" every weekend and I have become quite familiar with these parishes. As a senior priest, I notice the variety of ways the Sunday Eucharist is done, and there is a variety.

Theresa Doyle

My husband and I are Canadian. We live across the river from Michigan, twenty minutes away from St. Christopher Parish where I worked. We experience liturgy in a number of parishes in Canada—our home cluster of parishes and parishes where my married children live but do not attend. I also have participated in parish Sunday liturgies in Michigan, Ohio, Florida, Pennsylvania, New Jersey, Colorado, California, Indiana—places where I have presented workshops over the years. I also notice different practices at the liturgy.

"WE" AND "THEY"

Our experience of so many parishes is that, by and large, parishes do try to make the people feel part of the Sunday celebration but often the people are not treated as Church. Examples follow.

Before the liturgy begins, several parishes have a commentator saying something like this, *"Good morning, Welcome to St. _____."* The impression given to people seems to be that they are not the Church; they are not the parish. Somebody else is welcoming them to the parish. Perhaps, a welcome could be given to visitors to the parish. However, visitors who are baptized already belong to the Church and are not strangers.

We notice a different practice that is fairly common and better expresses who we are as Church. Before the opening hymn, people are asked to turn and greet each other and to introduce themselves. In this way of welcoming, the people themselves receive each other.

Sadly, many in the Church do not experience themselves as Church. In my experience of being a priest for fifty years, I find that the majority of faithful Mass-attending Catholics often speak of the Church as "they" rather than "we." For younger Catholics, it is even more so. Parishioners may have been told that they are the Church but often their self-recognition as Church is theoretical and vague. Telling people who they are (Church) does not convince for the most part. Treating parishioners as Church all the time, especially in the liturgy, has a better chance of convincing them over time.

Parishes can keep their people at a distance even as parishes try to bring people in. One parish we both know well ends its year with a dinner of appreciation for all who do the work of the parish. It is called the Volunteer Appreciation Dinner. The invitation reads, "We really appreciate all you do for us." Of course, volunteers are unpaid staff. But, somehow, the impression is that "volunteers" are in an outside position helping people called "we." In reality, baptized people in ministry are acting as Church and are not volunteers in someone else's organization. The baptized are the "we."

WHO ARE THE SPECIAL PEOPLE?

The special ones at the Eucharist are the assembled people themselves. All the particular ministries exist for their sake, to build them up.

The ministerial priesthood is at the service of the common priesthood. The ministerial priesthood is the means by which Christ unceasingly builds up and leads his Church. *CCC #1547*

The priest, deacons, and other liturgical ministers are part of the People of God, the Church gathered at the Sunday Eucharist.

For the celebration of the Eucharist is the action of the whole Church, and in it each one should carry out solely but totally that which pertains to him, in virtue of the place of each within the People of God. *GIRM #5*

The People of God, gathered around Christ, are the central focus at Mass. The priest presides but he is part of this gathered People of God. Keeping that central focus is not easy.

There still are parishes where the presider does not join in the singing. He may be giving the impression that he is not part of the People of God. We also notice that some presiders look more to the book than they look at the people giving the impression that we are not celebrating this Mass together.

However, the priest and the people have distinct roles in the liturgy. *The General Instruction of the Roman Missal* speaks of the "communion" between the priest and the people at Mass. Priest and people have distinct roles but the distinction does not separate priest from people and people from priest.

The dialogues between priest and faithful and the acclamations are of great significance, for they are not simply outward signs of communal celebration but *foster and bring about communion* between priest and people. *GIRM #34*

An example of this dialogue between priest and people came home to me at St. Christopher Parish where I had been pastor. I always sang the doxology and then joined the people in singing the great Amen. I always did that until the music director informed me that the Amen belongs to the congregation and I was taking the response of the people. My role was to invite their response and then listen to receive their response. At one parish where I now assist on weekends, I notice the pastor making my mistake. He sings with the people their great Amen, thinking he is supporting them by joining in. As I learned, we presiders are asked to respect and honor the people we are gathered with and we have to expect the people to do their acclamations.

In one of our small rural parishes, the church has a substantial solid wooden barrier that separates the music group section from the rest of the people. The choir has eight to ten people but occupies space for three times that number. That barrier closes off their area, even at the two Masses without the choir. Music ministers certainly need a reserved space but not so prominent a space and one that prevents parishioners from coming closer to the altar and ambo.

In another close-knit church community, the altar servers don't sing. Their trainer never told them that this is an expected part of serving and is as important as the mechanical things they do. Those running the parish do not seem to notice the lack of singing in the servers. It does not bother them that this special group doing a particular ministry is not part of the most special group, the congregation as it sings its prayer.

At a different parish we both know, a young high school cantor with a beautiful voice sometimes sings an inspiring piece before Mass. We all applaud. A neighboring community sometimes has the children come forward after Communion to perform a song. Again, we applaud. The thinking goes: how could we not clap for these beautiful young ones and wouldn't this help keep them and their young parents coming? Calling attention to special people or to special ministries can take the focus from the assembled Body of Christ. It easily puts people into the audience mode and keeps them passive. In our example of the children's piece right after communion, the people's attention goes away from who we are together in this sacred moment.

Neither of us is against applauding at Mass—on some occasions. For example: recognizing a couple who have lived the sacrament of marriage for the People of God and are renewing their wedding vows on their 50th. A further example could be applauding someone who, at that Mass, was newly baptized into Christ and into the Body of Christ, which we are. Applauding in such occasions keeps the focus on the people gathered because these "special" people are living the sacraments we all share.

The most frequent appreciation I hear from many parishioners is how much they love "my Mass." Somehow in the deeper consciousness of many Catholics, the reality that Christ and the Body of Christ—all of us—are doing the Eucharist has not caught on. I also hear priests of different age groups still speaking about "their" Mass.

PUTTING THE MASS ON — FOR THE PEOPLE

We find that there is a common perception that the Sunday Eucharist is put on for the people coming. It is as if we people come to something being done and we listen and observe and hope to get "something out of this." This attitude of making the Mass happen for the people can get lodged into the minds of liturgical ministers and presiders. We find that many Catholics—good faithful practicing ones—still see the Liturgy as being "put on" for them or being done for them. So many come looking mainly for the uplift from music performed for them or from the message in the homily.

Several parishes we experience give instructions to people to "please stand" or "please be seated." It is as if someone is directing the assembly or inviting them to what is theirs by right. A better environment happens when the people respond more naturally and they themselves assume their roles in the Liturgy. The word Liturgy actually means the work of the people. The point is to treat people as Church allowing them to take their rightful place. The Church at the Eucharist is the priest and people dialoging back and forth, responding to the Lord, celebrating more spontaneously and not under direction.

To both of us, the immediate way we notice that the people are observers at Mass is that they do not sing, especially they do not sing the acclamations. Our experience of so many parishes is that people at Mass may say the prayers together but are not joined together in the sung responses. There are many reasons for this lack, the main one simply may be that North Americans come to the Eucharist largely as individuals. Yet, singing brings people together as nothing else does. It expresses heartfelt prayer and gives expression to ourselves as Church.

Why are parish leaders not disturbed by this lack and why are they not driven to keep addressing this passivity of so many at Mass? Is it because parish leaders do not think the song of the people is critically important to the celebration of the Eucharist? The mentality of putting on the Liturgy for people rather than bringing people into the action might explain a lot.

For example, one parish in the area has female cantors who lead songs and the responsorial psalm at a pitch and volume that keep people from singing, especially keeping men from singing. Some song leaders are so close to the microphone that their voices are heard over the voice of the congregation. In several parishes we know, the acclamations simply do not seem familiar to the assembly.

In only one or two parishes have we noticed the majority of parishioners really singing the refrain of the psalm after the first reading or really singing the great Amen. Rarely have we seen any parish where the cantor steps back from the microphone and soften his or her voice to be only a little support to the congregation. It is vital that people hear each other's voices. When they do not, the expression of Church is weaker.

Our final point about parishes we are working with is the practice of adding extras to their liturgies to make people feel important. One parish actually has the pastor distributing fresh roses after the homily on Mother's Day. There was applause for the oldest mother. Then more applause for the youngest mother. Beautiful and heart-warming, perhaps, but again it seems the focus is taken from the living word just addressed to the whole people.

Every word of the liturgy is important and needs to be heard, including the sending rite. Some parishes add prayers before the final hymn, for example, the Prayer to St. Michael or the Hail Mary. The additions take the focus from Christ's words sending his people forth and put the focus on good but misplaced devotion. This same breaking of attention happens at a parish when the announcements go on for too long.

We may seem to be making a fuss over small practices in the liturgy. In some of these examples, maybe we are. Still, our point is about always keeping focus. None of this is criticism of the good intentions behind these common practices in parishes. Many of the added extras to the celebration of the Eucharist were intended to welcome and affirm people, but we do not need the additions. The liturgy itself can do that and more.

People slowly will begin to believe that we are the Church together—priest and people—when the liturgy itself treats and expects Church to act as Church. However, if people are to be convinced of the importance of preparing themselves for Mass before they come, that convincing certainly must be reinforced by valuing them as the People of God when they do come.

Keep the Focus. Christ himself is the main celebrant and agent in the celebration of the Eucharist. Notice where the gaze of Christ stays! He gives his undivided attention and unconditional love to the people he has called and brought together. He himself speaks his word to them in order to draw them into communion and then he sends them to bring that communion into his world. The priest acts *in persona Christi*. It seems to us that one simple way to be in the person of the Lord is to look at the people the way the Lord looks at them: as his body, his bride that he loves more than his own life. Much clearer focus happens in the liturgy when the presider simply conveys Christ's joy because each person decided to accept the invitation to come.

Looking at the Sunday Eucharist at your parish:

> How is the focus on God's People gathered together? Try to name specifics.
>
> What practical things would make that focus better?
>
> Who look like the "special" people at the liturgy?

Chapter Four
SUNDAY EUCHARIST'S CHALLENGE:
THE WAY PARISHIONERS ARE LIVING TODAY

Do not conform yourself to this age but be transformed by the renewal of your mind.
Romans 12:2

If how we "do Mass" affects the dispositions people need in order to be transformed by the Word, the culture affects those dispositions even more. When the People of God come to the Sunday Eucharist, they come already heavily influenced by the culture into which they are immersed all week. The prevailing culture is an ocean we all swim in. It is like the air we breathe, all the time forming our attitudes and values often without our realizing it.

The Constitution on the Sacred Liturgy says that **"When the Scriptures are read in Church; it is Christ himself speaking to his people."** Christ himself is speaking his powerful word to form his people according to his own mind and heart. So, why is that word so often not heard? Why is the transformation so little in evidence? There are many reasons but all the reasons come down to one basic cause. For the people to take the gospel to heart and be transformed by the Sunday Eucharist, people must be ready to hear and be transformed. The culture makes that difficult.

THE SOCIAL ENVIRONMENT—
AROUND US AND IN US, CONSTANTLY

As we have presented workshops in various parts of the U.S. and Canada, we have asked a simple question at least forty times: "How is life different for people today compared to a generation or two generations ago?" People (over the age of forty) have no trouble answering from their own experience and their answers converge into common patterns:

- People are very busy and on the go constantly.
- Relationships in families are lessened.
- Families are single-parented, blended—different.
- Both parents work leaving less time for family.
- There is a huge impact of media of all kinds.
- Constant stimulation is the norm.
- Real and deep communication has given way to texting, Facebook, Twitter.
- There is mistrust of all institutions, including the Church.
- More fear.
- People are on their own, trying to figure things out.

Older people are quite aware that we are different than we were. Life and the pace of life are different enough from the past that the parish has to find ways to form its people that work more effectively for today.

One of our parish experiences illustrates modern culture and its huge impact. It comes from a St. Christopher Parish Confirmation retreat for 9th graders. On the second day of the retreat, each young person was sent alone outdoors for twenty minutes of silence—no companions, no cell phones, no i-Pods. In the debriefing after the experience, many of the young people said that this was the first silence they had ever experienced. Others said it was the longest period of silence in their entire lives. These young people have not been given the gift of silence and a time to become still—not doing something or listening to something. This inability to be in silence is not just an issue with young people. How many adults know that quiet in their lives is necessary to hear the voice of God? This is not a gift prized in today's world.

Our second observation comes from an older priest who has seen a lot over his many years as a pastor. It is from his parish bulletin for the feast of SS. Peter and Paul.

Selling the Church Today

In the U.S. culture, everything is measured by individual choice. We are taught that it is our right to choose everything and anything in our lives. The individual accepts or rejects things or people according to his tastes and preferences. In the culture built almost totally on the individual, the Church suffers because the Church is communal and not just individual.

In a culture of "what I get out of it" or "what's in it for me", the Catholic Church is hard to sell. Because people today are so disconnected from each other and from their past, the Catholic connections are not easily appreciated. Many look to mega churches and community churches with stimulating preachers. To truly be a living member of the Catholic Church takes a little more work. It means to step out of today's individualistic culture to join with millions and millions of people over century after century. There is a whole value system and a reverence for life, which comes from a Catholic heart. Many in the Church have not gotten past the externals and the rules and remain psychologically on the outside of the Church even though they happen to be Catholic. The challenge for every one of us is to find out why we do what we do as the Church—to find the reasons behind our rituals and rules. Being Catholic is about connections, the connection with Jesus Christ and the connections with each other in and through him.

THE CULTURAL SHIFT IN PARISH ITSELF

For American and Canadian parishioners, the experience of parish itself has changed a great deal over the last two generations. The parish is less and less the center for social life, neighborhood identity, education, sports and recreation. In reality, the parish today has less effect on people's lives and everyday values. And, the parish must compete for people's time, constantly. Surveys consistently show that American and Canadian Catholics are coming to have most of the same attitudes and values as the rest of society.

A SELF-SUFFICIENT HUMANISM

By and large, our parishioners coming on Sunday are "on the go" all week, often with stressful responsibilities. Many are stimulated by constant media throughout every day and have little silence in their lives. In a world of sixty-second sound bites and constant messaging, people find it difficult to concentrate very long on anything. Finally, this present society is becoming in many ways one of purely self-sufficient humanism. Many ordinary people live without any consciousness of God and find fulfillment only in this life. More and more, formerly religious people just live day by day.

How many Catholic parishioners also live this way where, except for an hour on Sunday, God does not factor in! People of faith are surrounded by neighbors, fellow workers, and family members who get along quite well without God.

Much of the recent research of religious attitudes is concluding that the most striking trend in American religion has been the growing percentage of adults who do not identify with any religious group ("nones"). And the vast majority of them (78%) say they were raised as a member of a particular denomination before giving it up.

It is from this culture that the People of God come to Mass on Sunday.

CONTINUALLY FORMING THE PARISH
FORMING PARISH INTO A DELIBERATE COUNTER-CULTURE

The typical parish is not competing well with the culture in forming people's attitudes and mindset. Generally speaking, the parish, as we have it, is not working. The fact is that the one hour on Sunday does not form the majority of Catholic people in a life-changing way. For the majority of busy, over-extended, disconnected, non-reflective parishioners, there has to be something more than just showing up for the celebration of the Sunday Eucharist. Something is needed that prepares these parishioners for that Eucharist. There has to be a kind of alternative culture.

Forming an alternative culture does not mean a siege mentality of the Church against the world. God's Spirit is quite active in the modern world. There are movements toward harmony, greater recognition of inequalities in our systems, and the internet that makes possible a communication previously unheard of. But, there is much in the culture that impedes mindfulness and the deeper listening parishioners need to bring to the Eucharist.

That statement about the parish not working can be discouraging but it also can be encouraging. For one pastor we work with in the Cleveland Diocese, it is inspiring. Like so many, this priest was overwhelmed doing all the "necessary" programs and never felt he was good enough in all of his constant hard work. He says it was freeing to hear that it is not working. He now still works very hard but he is focused on putting in place parish structures that create a culture where people can encounter Christ in a personal and communal way.

For as pervasive and all-encompassing as the secular culture is, the abiding presence of Christ in the Sunday Eucharist celebration can persuade his people differently. His word is effective and is able to recreate anyone's heart. However words only affect a person when there is an active listener: willing to engage with the words, connect the words to one's own life experience, and make personal decisions because of what is heard.

For those of us who lead parishes, our job is to give people the means to become those active listeners to the Word of the Lord (spoken most authentically in the Church's Eucharist) before they come to Mass. We believe that leaders are being called to provide ways for parishioners to knit together to form an alternate culture able to slow down and to listen. But before we present details on forming that alternate culture, we have one more chapter on the centrality of Sunday Eucharist as the only way to lasting renewal.

As you observe your own family members and professional contacts;

> Where do you see the Church making the difference for the way people view life or make everyday decisions?
>
> Where is it not?

Chapter Five
THE PARISH SUNDAY EUCHARIST

...that the love with which you loved me may be in them and I in them.

John 17:26

The unity of the Mystical Body: The Eucharist makes the Church! *CCC #1396*

Our experience every Sunday at Mass is not just the most important thing we do: it is what we do. The parish exists for the Eucharist.

> **Mother Church earnestly desires that all the faithful be led to that full, conscious, and active participation in liturgical celebrations which is demanded by the very nature of the liturgy. In the restoration and promotion of the sacred liturgy, this full and active participation by all the people is the aim to be considered before all else; for it is the primary and indispensable source from which the faithful are to derive the true Christian spirit. Therefore, through the needed program of instruction, pastors of souls must zealously strive to achieve it in all their pastoral work.**
> *Constitution on the Sacred Liturgy #14*

The Church sees the Eucharist so very basic because it is there that Christ directly forms his Body— more and more deeply, Sunday by

Sunday. All he needs is receptivity. The focus of all pastoral work is to bring people to the liturgy ready for that full and conscious participation. This preparation is the "aim to be considered before all else."

Isn't that what the Church is saying by calling the Mass **"the summit toward which the activity of the Church is directed"** and **"the fountain from which all her power flows"**? This idea of the Eucharist being the "source and summit" of everything in the parish has to be more than an idea or a theory. Somehow, that goal must drive how we actually do everything else in the parish.

Why not let this become the overriding goal by which to measure everything happening in the parish: bringing the people of the Church to the Eucharist in such a way that they experience Christ more consciously. Experiencing Christ! It is his own word he is speaking and, by his own word, bringing us to communion with himself and so with each other and finally beyond our gathering to his world. A successful parish can be honed and disciplined toward preparing for and celebrating that Mass. However in our observations, most parishes are not so deliberately focused.

What is asked of the people, including the priest, coming on Sunday? Do they know they are expected to bring something more than merely showing up?

> **To respond to this invitation, we must prepare ourselves for so great and so holy a moment.** *CCC #1385*

When I gave this quote to some daily communicants in my parish in Sarnia, Canada; they said they had never heard this nor did they know they were supposed to prepare for Mass. Who tells people they are expected to prepare and who shows them how to prepare?

HOW WE COME TO MASS

The two of us believe that the following descriptions of how American and Canadian Catholics come to Mass fit most parishes and most parishioners.

First of all, most North Americans come to Mass largely as individuals. After all, we come from a pervasively individualistic culture. The pastor's bulletin article quoted earlier says it well.

Most of us come to the liturgy not consciously connected to the other people present, the world Church, to those gone before us in death and or to the saints.

Many at the liturgy might believe, at least in their better moments, they are valuable to God but perceiving they are valuable to the Church is another matter. Few of us would know - "in our guts" - that the Church actually needs us beyond our money or getting involved in some parish program; but rather that we personally matter. Most do not see that their absence at Mass would make the Church eminently poorer without them there. Does one's life experience or one's personal struggles make any real difference for who we are as Church? The majority of Catholics would not have ever considered such a question.

Secondly, for the vast majority, the scriptures spoken at Mass are heard there for the first time that week. There has been no engagement with that word before Mass. There will be no interaction with that word after Mass. And, for all of us, that word spoken by Christ himself can easily become like a drop in the sea of words coming at us all week long.

Thirdly, most people at Mass have not prepared for that liturgy beforehand. They do not even know that this is expected of them.

Parishioners, by and large, would not know that they are expected to bring their lives to Mass, to hand over at least something from their lives to Christ, and to let him take them with himself to the Father. To review one's life over the week and deliberately and consciously choose what one will offer is necessary preparation most of us do not do before coming.

Finally, very few Mass attendees would have shared that Sunday's gospel and its connections to their life experience with anyone nor would most know how to do so.

A people can be transformed when they are aware and come to trust the person who tells them the truth about who they really are. For the Church, that person is Christ at the Eucharist. How we come to Mass either places great limits on what Christ can do for us and in us or it can help Christ greatly. The challenge to pastors and all parish pastoral workers is helping people to come with the right dispositions.

With all these limitations, what can we do to make those gathering on Sunday more aware of Christ present, more attuned to what he is saying and doing right now, and more responsive to him? Continually keeping that question uppermost in mind is the most important step in forming the parish.

WE HAVE BARELY BEGUN

Getting people's attention and keeping their attention is no easy matter these days. In our fast-paced and technologically driven world, people generally do not stay focused for long on one person or on one image. They move on to the next and then the next.

Parishes themselves are not always helpful at liturgy. The presider can distract by calling attention to himself---to his personality or to his humor. As already mentioned, the music ministers can become performers. Extra additions at Mass can also distract. Having many attention getters can take people's focus from the Person at the center of the celebration and from our responsibility to respond to him.

We certainly have made some first steps. We have begun to move from thinking of "Father's Mass" to the Mass being the work of the assembly and finally to the Mass being primarily Christ's action inviting his people to join him. Keeping our worship spaces simple and uncluttered without looking cold and sterile also has begun.

That same simplicity and focus have been slower in coming when we look at how liturgy is done. There still are too many words spoken to people inundated with words all the time. The homily often is about a message and a theme drawn from three readings rather than about drawing people into the very presence of the Word made flesh. The seven places for silence in the Sunday liturgy may not be honored. It is easy in the liturgy to give little recognition that Christ is the main celebrant and provider.

Changes to the liturgy are necessary and Volume 2 will speak to some of those, including homilies, explanations before certain parts of the liturgy, etc. But external practices alone are not enough for people to be transformed. Something else has to happen and that something must be the way people come to Mass—their dispositions. Pastors are beginning to see that the "full, conscious, and active participation" of the people in the liturgy is much more than getting everybody friendly and singing.

Until we truly receive the Word and the Word finds a home in us, our transformation in Christ is quite limited. We are convinced that the greatest change the parish needs is to bring as many parishioners as possible together regularly, in smaller groupings, to help each other connect their everyday lives to the faith of the Church expressed at Mass.

> How does your parish help prepare people for the upcoming Sunday Mass? How do you prepare?
>
> At your parish's Sunday Eucharist, what are the specifics that move people's minds and hearts toward Christ as the center? What distracts?

Chapter Six
THE PARISH STRUCTURED FOR THE EUCHARIST

My Sheep hear my voice.

John 10:27

Every parish already has one central activity forming the parish and that is the Sunday Eucharist. What Christ Jesus is doing in the Eucharistic celebration is fashioning his Body, the Church. (See the CCC #1325)

> **But, in order that the liturgy may be able to produce its full effects, it is necessary that the faithful come to it with proper dispositions, that their minds should be attuned to their voices, and that they should cooperate with divine grace lest they receive it in vain.**
> *Constitution on the Sacred Liturgy #11*

If the Sunday Eucharist is the main way Christ is forming his people as Church, then everything else happening in the parish can become a means to help him do his work. Every program, activity, and committee meeting somehow can get us to the next Eucharist a little more aware of what Christ is doing and more open to his action. It seems to follow that all parish activities would be evaluated on how they are helping the Sunday celebration become the source and summit of everything else.

Is it possible to reorient the entire body of parishioners toward the Eucharist so totally and still keep the parish the same? Our experience says no.

EUCHARIST AT THE CENTER
NOT ANOTHER PROGRAM

Just adding a program about the Eucharist is not enough. A program cannot provide the continual and sustained environment necessary to keep parishioners aware of who they are, especially as they are gathered together on Sunday. We think what is needed is not a single program but that all the existing programs be done in such a way so that parishioners continually are preparing for the upcoming liturgy.

The Sunday liturgy is supposed to send people out with a different mindset than the culture offers. When you look at how culturally-conditioned people are, is a sixty-minute liturgy each week enough to change us? Look at your own parish to answer that question. Speak to family members no longer coming to Mass. Look at Catholic people who have joined fundamentalist or community churches because they "find Christ there." So many have left never realizing what the Eucharist is, never experiencing Christ in any kind of personal way at Mass. The two of us have experienced that there is a way a parish can celebrate Sunday so people begin to experience the Mass as the high point of their week. And, it begins with the word Christ proclaims each Sunday.

Throughout the Scriptures, the word of God is shown as God actually doing something, making something new happen. By his word, God creates the universe out of chaos, brings his Israelites back from exile and reveals some of his own heart by giving the law to his people. The same effective life-changing word of God actually is spoken by Christ at Mass.

Christ is present in his word, since it is He Himself who speaks when the holy Scriptures are read in the church.
Constitution on the Sacred Liturgy #7

In many cases, however, Christ's word does not get into many parishioners at Mass. Much less does his word remain in people continually forming their perceptions about themselves and all the events of their lives. Why? Many at Liturgy do not approach the word as a living word spoken right now by Christ and addressed to us. So, people come looking for a good message, hoping for something they can take home for inspiration and meaning. Notice how differently Jesus presents his word and the desired outcome for his word. For him, his word is more than a good message about something.

> *Whoever loves me will keep my word, and my Father will love him, And we will come to him and make our dwelling with him.*
> *John 14:23*

For Jesus, it's about communion with us. For Christ and ourselves remaining and abiding in each other means both parties must continually be present to each other. So, the parish's main task is to make every effort to get its parishioners fully conscious and present at Mass to the One who is really and truly present to them.

The readings are spoken to us in the present by Jesus Christ himself. Just that single awareness would make a great difference in parishes—knowing the Lord is talking now.

Two parishes where I help on the weekends have the lectors read an introduction giving some historical and cultural background before they do the actual readings. This can be helpful, even necessary. For many (most), the first reading at Mass comes from nowhere. The majority of people don't know who the patriarchs are, what the exile is all about, the temple's importance, David's role, Jewish sacrifice rituals, and that biblical prophets don't necessarily foretell future events. More importantly, a lot of parishioners don't realize all these Old Testament promises point to Christ and that we are meant to find hope in those promises right now. However, in these two parishes the introductions are all about past history and what people were facing back then. Parishioners say they like these informational explanations before the readings. "Interesting," they say. But, how are people being helped to attend to the reading itself as the active word being spoken directly to them here and now?

The other great obstacle to our hearing that personal word of Christ comes from the way society continually shapes us. With constant busyness and constant media, our parishioners have words coming at them all the time. As a result, the attention span of modern people seems to be getting shorter. The words of Jesus Christ get lost among so many words.

Possibly the greatest challenge for Sunday is the consumer society--as ours certainly is. In such a society, people often do not feel they personally matter. How many at the Sunday Eucharist even hear an intimate word during a typical week? Yet in the liturgy, they are expected to hear God's word as a personal and intimate word.

No simple parish program added to everything else going on will change all of these influences. Practically then, how can the living word of Jesus Christ get into the majority of people at the Sunday Eucharist? The parish will have to direct its attention and its energies toward this one direction of truly hearing and responding and will have to stay focused in that one direction. The parish itself must be different. It must be structured differently.

We have experienced that very change in the parish; the change that affects the way all the programs are done. Rather than having good programs co-exist side by side, all programs are unified by the one clear and conscious purpose of the parish. In this systemic approach to parish, there is one ultimate goal for every existing program: bit by bit, to bring people to the Sunday liturgy more ready to engage with the word.

TWO PERMANENT STRUCTURES FOR PARISH

To recap: Christ makes the Church happen; we don't. Only his word calls the Church into being. For those in charge of parishes, the task is to bring parishioners together so they can become more attentive to his word and respond to his word.

> **Pastors of souls must, therefore, realize that, when the liturgy is celebrated, more is required than the mere observance of the laws governing valid and licit celebration. It is the duty of pastors also to ensure that the faithful take part knowingly, actively, and fruitfully."**
> *Constitution on the Sacred Liturgy #11*

CONTINUALLY FORMING THE PARISH

We believe parishioners need to be given a way to help each other hear God's word and make everyday life connection with that word. If parishioners' hearing each other's faith is so important, how can it happen unless pastoral leadership provides a structure to help people hear the Scriptures the way the Church hears the Scriptures.

The Lord speaks his word most fully to the Church at the Eucharist. So, our process of getting people hearing and responding to his word at parish events and meetings becomes a kind of training for that upcoming liturgy. Getting the parish ready for Sunday in all its activities will require sustained effort and purposeful organization. From our work throughout North America, we have found over and over that ordinary pastors and parish leaders are quite capable of doing this.

From our own experience and from the experience of many other parishes, we are convinced that the parish will need new permanent structures:

- to slow parishioner's lives down
- to get them to reflect on their lives as they hear Christ in Sunday's gospel and
- to come together with a few others to listen and speak to each other.

These new structures, above all, help parishioners deepen their self-perception as being personally formed by Christ and connected to the Church Christ is bringing together on Sunday. To this end, we are advocating the structuring of parish in two equally important and necessary ways to help the parish keep the Eucharist as its source and summit.

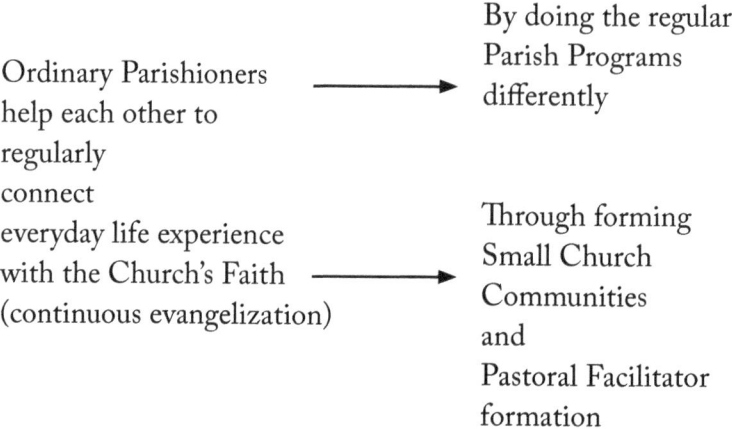

DOING EVERYTHING DIFFERENTLY

Doing the regular parish programs differently means that every activity, committee and organization is structured so there is:

- time to hear the Church's faith
- some time for a faith/life reflection question (or a few questions)
- some quiet time
- a little time to listen to each other in small groups of two or three.

By the "Church's faith" we usually mean giving people the opportunity to hear together the upcoming Sunday Gospel. (On occasion, it may not work to use the Sunday gospel so another Scripture or another kind of reflection would be used that is a better fit. However the same following process would be used.) After listening as the gospel is read slowly and reverently, the next step is to give people a little time to connect that gospel to their own lives by one or several experiential questions. Finally, spend time speaking to and listening to one other person just for a few minutes—no more.

We provide these questions, commentary and prayer response for the upcoming Sunday gospel on the National Alliance of Parishes Restructuring into Communities (NAPRC) website, **www.naprc.net**.

It will take time to insert such a format into every parish event and gathering. This reflection and sharing may not be familiar or immediately comfortable for everyone, including pastoral leaders. In our experience, we found it very helpful to use simple "non-churchy" language and questions that are thoughtful but allow people to share at the level they choose.

At St. Christopher's Parish, it took us time to implement and find acceptance of this gospel hearing-reflecting-sharing model. We found only occasional resistance, especially when we first asked people to try the process. The resistance mostly came because this was new and unfamiliar. Over time, however, this model simply became the way we did things. What follow are a couple of instances where acceptance took a little more time.

The parish grounds were weeded, mulched and planted each year by any parishioners willing to show up on a Saturday morning and work for an hour or two. The one parishioner organizing the work bought the mulch, the bushes and plants, and provided the refreshments. She had been the boss of this project for several years and her personality was very task-oriented. As the workers came together, we asked people to take a moment with the question "What would you like the people of the parish to experience when they come to church and look at these grounds?" Then, we repeated the question. We had intended that people would pause with the question and then some would speak. But the boss said immediately, "We didn't come here for that. We have work to do." The two of us had to stand our ground and politely say the work will get done, but we need to help each other see that the purpose of our work is to provide a beautiful place for God's people to gather, and that the outside of our church should point to the great action of God that takes place inside. Then, we posed our question again and heard a few responses. Each year after that it got easier to start the work with some kind of reflection.

The other example of a challenge to me as the pastor was the parish Finance Council. It had met for years with an opening Our Father and then on to business. I introduced the idea of the gospel reflection and its purpose. I asked them to try the process for a few meetings, making sure it took only about twelve minutes of the meeting time. A long-standing and key member of the Finance Council began to come late so as to miss the new prayer format. I had to meet with him privately to ask for his support for this "new way" and give him further reasons. He reluctantly cooperated and eventually the process itself won him over.

Over time and with dogged persistence, the culture of the parish changed because of doing the regular parish programs differently. This first structure we call "coloring the parish."

> *"I am impressed by the growth of our small church communities but I am most interested in and anxious to see a change in the way everything we do in the parish is centered on helping each other hear the gospel."*
>
> Father Charles Klinger,
> pastor of St. Paul the Apostle Parish,
> Westerville, OH

COLORING THE PARISH

The following are some of the ways St. Christopher's Parish began to do differently the everyday activities that usually are happening in every parish. The consistent question for every parish event is this: How can these parishioners here and now help each other look at their lives or look at this event through the lens of the Sunday gospel?

The upcoming gospel always is the preferred reflection and focus. But as mentioned earlier, if using the gospel for the upcoming Sunday did not fit certain particular situations, we found other ways to help parishioners hear the faith of the Church.

- Every standing committee or parish work group hears the Sunday gospel. Then, the group spends a little quiet time with a few simple life questions based on the Gospel, and each person shares with one or two others. The time ends with prayer for the parish or other intentions. Even the Parish Finance Council (and the money-counting group) uses this format.

- Each sacramental prep meeting with parents and/or children uses some kind of faith sharing based on the topic at hand. There always is some form of a prayer experience to conclude the meeting. For example, at a Confirmation prep meeting: we mixed the parents and 8th graders into small groups of three to four. We made sure the students were not with their own parents. The seven gifts of the Holy Spirit, along with the opposite traits of each gift, were listed. Each small group was given one particular gift and asked to describe in as much detail as possible a person from their experience whose life expresses that gift. Then, each group reported to all of us. To conclude the meeting, there always was some form of a prayer experience for each to respond to what they heard God saying.

- Every rehearsal (wedding, 1st Communion, Confirmation, graduation) includes some kind of faith reflection and question on the event, a time to speak to one person, and a few responses shared in the large group. Before wedding practices, for example, the friends and the family present make a circle around the bride and groom. All are asked to consider this couple prayerfully and reflect on what they would need from God for a good and lasting marriage. After 30 seconds or so, the leader speaks aloud some very simple gift and asks the others to say something. There always have been responses by the people present. All join hands around the couple and pray the Our Father.

- Testimonies, done simply by down-to-earth ordinary parishioners at parish celebrations, help others to reflect on the faith of the Church. At the annual breakfast after the Mass for the high school graduates, a senior boy and a senior girl give a short witness on the importance of faith in their personal lives. At the Mass itself, there is a personal reflection given by a previous graduate on their faith experience during college and/or on embarking upon a career. Often, the people present are asked to consider for a moment something they would take for themselves from the talks.

- The religious education program gives students a copy of the upcoming Sunday gospel written in age-appropriate language. Along with the gospel are two or three questions for parents and children to talk over.

- At baptisms, outside of Mass, the people present are given a card and a pen. Friends and family write a short letter to the infant or child about to be baptized. The letter says "My prayer for you on the day of your baptism is . . ." Each one reads his or her letter to the person next to them. Then, a few read their letters aloud to the Church. With this practice over the years, I have seen people express, even though haltingly, the Church's faith about this sacrament.

- Training Liturgical Ministers (altar sever training, lectors, extra ordinary ministers of the Eucharist, hospitality ministers) always includes a question around the ministry itself and not simply the mechanics. For example, the high school student and the adult doing the server training always begin each of the three training sessions with a question and then have each person speaking and listening to one or two others on that question: "What difference would you like your serving to make for your own life? How do your praying and singing affect the other people at Mass? In what ways can you prepare yourself before you come to church so you can pay better attention to Christ here?"

- The ministers to the homebound meet three times a year for formation. They always speak to each other around definite questions that tie their ministry to the work of the Church. "What does the Church want to communicate to the homebound or sick person? What gift does the homebound person bring to the rest of the parish? In what ways can we help the rest of the parish be aware of the homebound and what they bring to us? What does your homebound person need us (the parish) to pray for?"

- Letters promising prayers for those preparing for Confirmation or to be received into the Church are a way of expressing the Church's faith. These letters are asked of parishioners, including homebound parishioners.
- Every parish gathering has some way to learn each other's names, at least one person's name. There always is some way to listen and to speak in a faith perspective.

Many parishioners will not get into a small community, at least right away. But, this process of reflection and listening in every parish program gives some of the experience of a small community's format. Parishioners begin to grow in awareness of Christ now forming the Church. Persevering in this structure of doing all parish programs and events differently helped to change our parish culture. It had an ongoing effect that was cumulative, continually reinforcing, and built into the fabric of the parish. The gospel of Sunday began to get into parishioners more deeply than ever before. A pastor in the Archdiocese of Detroit calls this process "creating a gospel culture."

Another pastor says,
"I now see the whole week as an extended liturgy of the Word with as many as possible reflecting and sharing on the Gospel before Sunday. Not just activities, meetings, and groups but at home. We have to get the Word and practices of faith back into the home."
Father Jarlath Cunnane, Archdiocese of Los Angeles

We have noticed that parishioners in sacramental preparation programs for their children begin to be motivated toward a personal faith when they hear other adults share honestly and simply. The faith witness of other parents, especially men, impacts in ways that presentations or videos do not. One high school graduate wrote, "Thank you for helping me grow up knowing how important my faith is. Every week at Mass you would plant a seed, a question that would keep me thinking about God. This is something that will always stay with me."

This same graduate's father was only baptized. His own parents divorced when he was a child. His stepfather was kind and caring but was without faith of any kind. As a result, this grad's father never was raised in the Church. Now that he had three children of his own, his wife insisted on their Catholic upbringing. But, Church was like a foreign land where this dad was a stranger. He felt left out and unfamiliar with so much about the Church. It seemed like everybody else knew everything and he knew nothing—until he got to the meetings for parents preparing their children for the sacraments. At the sacramental programs for his children, he heard over and over the ways other regular parents (like himself) took a relationship with Christ seriously. He heard other men speak about trying to be more aware at Mass and listening—and often failing. Over the many years, this father began to see that personal faith as a Catholic was possible for himself and could make the difference in his life—like it did for others who spoke up. Because of the faith witness he experienced in sacramental programs for his children, he entered the RCIA process, eventually made a parish men's retreat and is now in a small church community. Much more happened for him because the sacramental programs were not simply child-centered or the communication of information through lecture. Most importantly, he heard the faith of other ordinary parents.

Like this father, there are so many parishioners needing a forum to hear the real faith, life struggles and joys of other young parents.

> When you experience a typical meeting or activity in your parish, do you find parishioner's personal faith strengthened or deepened?
>
> How about for yourself in those parish situations? Is your own awareness of God sharpened?
>
> How does your parish make it possible for ordinary parishioners to slow down their lives enough to become reflective and actually hear the gospel as the living Word?

Chapter Seven
SMALL CHURCH COMMUNITIES

The sower sows the word.
Those sown on rich soil are the ones who hear the word
and accept it
and bear fruit thirty and sixty and a hundred-fold.
Mark 4:14, 20

We have seen and experienced a tried and true way to cultivate that better soil for the Word of God to penetrate and have effect. It is about forming the people coming to Sunday Mass in such a deliberate way that they become a receptive environment. Then, the Word proclaimed will do its work.

All our parishes world-wide use the same altar missal for Mass. In the front of that missal is an introduction by Pope Paul VI. In a few paragraphs, the pope pulls together basic foundations that come from the Vatican II documents and the General Introduction to the *1st Edition of Roman Missal*. Paul VI's words could be seen as a summary of what the Church wants for its people.

> **All these things (the reformed Order of the Mass and the expanded Scripture readings at the liturgy) have been arranged in this way so as to arouse more and more among Christ's faithful that hunger for the Word of God by which, under the guidance of the Holy Spirit, the people of the New Covenant can be seen, as it were, to be impelled towards the perfect unity of the Church. We trust that given this arrangement both**

> **priests and faithful may make more devout spiritual preparation for the Lord's Supper and that, meditating more deeply on Sacred Scripture, they will be nourished more abundantly each day by the words of the Lord. In consequence, in accord with the teachings of the Second Vatican Council, Sacred Scripture will be regarded by all as an abiding fountain of spiritual life, as the principal basis for the handing on of Christian doctrine, and finally as the core of all theological formation.**
> *Paul VI Promulgation of the Roman Missal*

The challenge to prepare for Sunday comes strongly from the Church herself. It seems to us that the way the current society continually forms people makes the Church's challenge even more necessary.

Inserting gospel reflection and sharing questions into all parish programs begins a process so people at Mass can better hear and engage the Word of God. Yet, by itself this cannot mold the parish into a gospel culture. At parish committees and events, the time devoted to hearing and sharing the gospel is only 10-15 minutes. Also, most of the parishioners are not going to be involved in a parish event or committee. Even for the very involved, those meetings are occasional. We found that the parish needed to add another structure. A structure of small communities, where parishioners came together every week or every two weeks, for the sole purpose of spending time together with the gospel of Sunday.

The small church community (SCC) structure guided by trained facilitators connected to the pastor has proven to be the most effective way for the parish to do what Paul VI directs: **"arouse hunger for the Word of God, impel people toward the unity of the Church, help people devoutly prepare for Mass, and bring about personal meditation on the Lord's words so people are nourished each day with the Lord's guidance."**

There are parishes and dioceses worldwide that have already committed to small church communities connected to the Sunday Eucharist as their structure of renewal.

What we have come to know is there has to be a deliberate pastoral plan: a structure in the parish to form ongoing small church communities where parishioners are brought together in small groups of eight to twelve adults. Parishes may already have some smaller groupings of parishioners who share faith, such as bible study groups and post-Renew groups meeting around the Sunday Scriptures or men's and women's fellowship groups. And, didn't parishes do the "small group thing" back in the 1980s?

There are similarities and differences to what parishes have done in the past. Unlike previous small groups in some parishes, we see the present need is that the small church community is a permanent structure of the parish—not an occasional program or a movement for those wanting "that sort of thing." We are advocating something more than most existing small groups.

A NECESSARY RESPONSE TO THE CULTURE

The pervasive secular culture influences everybody all the time. Many church leaders are convinced a church culture can counter and compete for the minds and hearts of its people when that church culture also becomes more pervasive. Pope Benedict XVI (when he was still Cardinal Ratzinger) spoke forcibly by saying that the West could only be re-Christianized "by societies of spiritual concentration." In many parishes throughout the world, the small church communities are becoming those societies of spiritual concentration. They are permanent structures operating all the time, as the secular culture does. The small church communities are continuous and meet regularly week after week, year after year. The same people stay as members of the SCC and over time their comfort level with each other deepens. They continually help each other be attentive to the upcoming Sunday Gospel and use that Gospel as a lens to look at their everyday lives.

Any busy pastor or parish pastoral worker might jump to the practical questions, "How do you get people into these small groups and how do you keep people in these groups when their lives are already so busy?" Those questions are important and have to be addressed. However, right now, we would like to show how the SCCs actually make possible a very different way of life based upon values that are the reverse of the secular culture's values.

EUCHARIST AT THE CENTER

PRESENT ALL-ENCOMPASSING CULTURE	SMALL CHURCH COMMUNITY CULTURE
Self-sufficient humanism	God-directed humanism
Unfocused	Focused--Attentive to the Word
Fractured, interrupted consciousness (going from one thing to another)	"A long loving look at reality"
Superficial and temporary	Deep and lasting
Impersonal (consumer categories)	Personally, chosen and called by God
Inattentive /Individualistic	Communal. Formed as the Body of Christ.
Often divisive	"In Christ, all things hold together." *Col 1:17*
Unconnected/disconnected	Connected/reconnected
Image-driven (external) (how one comes across)	One's deeper personhood called and formed by God
Constant busyness Constant stimulation	Focused silence and quiet examination leading to a response
Consciousness primarily through social categories: race, ethnicity, income level	Consciousness through one's deeper Baptismal identity
One's worth by money, power, worldly success	One's worth as being continually created in God's image
React to situations and people	Respond to God revealing God's self in life-situations moment by moment

The two columns present a sharp contrast between two cultures. There is, of course, much good and much of God in the secular culture. Yet, it is clear there are very many deep-seated values present in Western society that severely limit people from being the good soil the Word of God can penetrate.

One example is our society's overly strong emphasis on human achievement, on "making something of oneself." A modern person's worth often is measured solely by level of income, physical appearance, job promotion. That same person, who happens to be a parishioner, comes to the Sunday Eucharist with such an identity deeply and continually reinforced. Over a life time, it is ingrained. Yet, God addresses his Word to people desiring to shape in them a different identity, a baptismal identity. This identity means a person is chosen and beloved before he or she can achieve anything and is held by God equally in both worldly successes and in failures. In the Eucharist, the Father speaks to sons and daughters. Sons and daughters conscious of their identity are able to hear. Which identity is the dominant one and which culture dominates the thinking of people at Mass?

Another example of the differing emphasis of the two cultures is our identity as Church. Media portrayals of the Catholic Church focus solely on its externals: its numbers, its waning influence on social issues, its scandals. In contrast, the Church sees its deepest reality as spiritual and from its spiritual base must acknowledge, own and address these issues. It is a community of persons bonded together by a shared Holy Spirit that outweighs all ethnic, racial, economic, and gender differences. Which culture seems to prevail in the attitudes of parishioners coming to the Sunday celebration? It seems to many in parish leadership that people come to Mass largely as individuals. They often seem to focus on externals much more than on the spiritual bond they have with each other.

Seeing everything only as individuals blocks parishioners from receiving the Word. The Word of God is addressed first of all to the community of the Church. As part of the community welcoming the Word, the individual then finds personal meaning. They come, as well, to know it is God calling the Church into existence by his Word.

The word "Church" designates the assembly of those whom God's Word "convokes," i.e., gathers together to form the People of God, and who themselves, nourished with the Body of Christ, become the Body of Christ. *CCC #777*

Simply put, the Church is a people called by God to be formed by God to be in Communion with God.

It is a pastoral challenge to get Catholics to become aware that God is calling them here and now to be Church. His Word gathers us together. His Word brings the Church into being and each of us is called into this creation of his. The small church community is the best means we have found to help parishioners move beyond individualism and to get a sense of Church. In the SCC, people hear the upcoming gospel in a communal setting. Together, they receive the gospel. They come to depend on God's Spirit enlightening each member of the group and learn to speak openly and honestly and to listen reverently to each other.

Many of us in pastoral leadership are concluding that the parish must structure itself as an alternative culture--a culture that gives the Word of God a much better chance of being heard as it is proclaimed on Sunday to the Church. This alternative culture will only happen through an intentional and deliberate effort.

> In what practical ways is your parish helping parishioners hear and take to heart the Word of God proclaimed on Sunday?
>
> What do you notice in our society that makes it difficult for people to open up to God's Word? What makes it difficult for you?

Chapter Eight

BUILDING THE PARISH FROM THE GROUND UP

> *Everyone who listens to these words of mine and acts on them will be like a wise man who built his house on rock.*
>
> Matthew 7:24

Along with many other pastoral leaders, we are promoting a different kind of parish, not a new program. We are about changing the way parishes operate.

Many programs to renew the parish add something new but continue everything already going on—all the committees, all the existing programs, all the ways parishioners are involved.

We are also about adding something new to the parish, small church communities. However, the SCCs are not simply an addition alongside everything else happening. These small communities are the building blocks of a new kind of parish. They are a structure upon which a new model of parish is being built. It is building the parish from the ground up.

> **The parish is not an outdated institution; precisely because it possesses great flexibility, it can assume quite different contours depending on the openness and missionary creativity of the pastor and the community.**
>
> Pope Francis *The Joy of the Gospel*. #28

Pope Francis encourages pastors and people to develop different parish "contours" so that "missionary creativity" can happen. In parishes world-wide, one of those contours is the development of the small church community. Ongoing small church communities with trained leaders connected to the pastor are a new structure. In these communities, people are helping each other to hear the gospel. The operative phrase is parishioners-helping-each-other. This clearly is "missionary creativity" because most of our parishioners never before spoke to anyone about their personal faith. What we saw happening was, for the first time, people began to hear the Gospel of the upcoming Sunday and reflect upon it as the way to look at their everyday lives. Over and over again, people told us they found courage and the language to begin expressing the faith in their families and in their workplaces because of their experience of the small community.

As more and more small church communities were formed in our parish, we noticed a change in the Sunday congregation at Mass. Visitors to the parish also commented that there was something distinctive at St. Christopher. It was something more than the homily or the music. There was a heart-felt reverence, attentiveness to the Word and a joy in being there. The people themselves were different.

The majority of parishioners were not in small church communities, only about 15-18% were. But, everyone at the weekend liturgies benefited from what the people in SCCs brought to the Sunday gathering. Everyone experienced being part of a deeper kind of community. As more and more parishioners (both those in SCCs and those not) were personally moved by the Word and drawn personally into union with the Word made flesh; they found a deeper relationship with the other parishioners at Mass. It became more real to parishioners that the bond they had with each other was because of the common bond they shared with Jesus Christ. The small church communities were the way we found to build the Church at the Sunday Eucharist from the ground up.

The small church communities did not become cliques or think of themselves as superior to those parishioners not in SCCs. This was for several reasons. First of all, the small community meetings were around the gospel which always speaks about God reaching out and including everyone, especially the forgotten ones. The second reason

CONTINUALLY FORMING THE PARISH

the small groups did not divide parishioners is the role of the pastoral leaders in each SCC. These leaders continually brought up the need to go out to the strangers and the people alone at Mass. Members of the small communities agreed not to sit together at the liturgy or to hang together before and after.

At our parish, parishioners began noticing each other and started becoming more considerate of each other. We do not mean that people were friendlier than before. They were always friendly. It was now more than simple friendliness. Parishioners slowly got used to reaching out to others at Mass, even to people they did not happen to know personally, simply because they became aware of their spiritual bond.

What we have seen over the twenty years time at St. Christopher's Parish is how the small church communities have created a much more aware Sunday assembly. People came to Mass more deeply formed, with a "deep religious sense" as the GIRM recommends for this holy people. It is very possible—and necessary—to build this kind of Eucharistic Community.

In every parish, young people and their children who still come to liturgy are experiencing the Church. The only Church most of them will know is the community around the Eucharist at their parish. For them, this is the Catholic Church. Will these young Catholics remain active church people if the Sunday community itself does not develop?

How we are together at the Eucharistic liturgy clearly speaks volumes. The community at Mass, people and priest joined, is the primary means of evangelization. We are what visitors, the occasional, and the regular attending parishioners experience. There they will see and experience faith, or the lack of it. We are the message as surely as the spoken words.

People at Mass make the effort to be there and that says a lot because most Catholics no longer make the effort. But, we know that parishes can do a better job of preparing parishioners for the Sunday Eucharist—not simply by adult education programs or Scripture study. There is need of a heart-felt realization from experience, of being a holy people. SCCs have proven to be a firm foundation for that realization.

The small church communities are not going to renew the parish. Every parish already has the program to transform its people. It is the celebration of the Sunday Eucharist. There we meet the Person who will rebuild the Church. It is the Word he speaks and the Communion he offers that transforms. The job of pastoral leadership is to bring to Jesus Christ a people attuned to his voice and themselves seeking communion. Our task is to get people to him. SCCs have proven to be the means to that end.

The Constitution on the Sacred Liturgy #7 states that Christ is truly present in his Word, in the person of the priest, in the Church gathered and under the Eucharistic species. Regular practicing Catholics certainly seem to appreciate Jesus' presence under the form of bread and wine. In most of the parishes we know and have served, there is a quiet and attentiveness at the Eucharistic Prayer, especially at the words of institution. And among Mass-attending Catholics, there still is a respect for the priest and people look for his leadership at Mass and for his homily.

But parishioners, by and large, often miss the two other ways Jesus Christ is with us. The Word is less appreciated as a living word being spoken right now by God personally. And his presence in the people gathered is even less appreciated.

In short, there seems to be a lack of awareness of coming into the presence of the Holy One during the entire Mass and not only in the liturgy of the Eucharist. Many people seem to lack the awareness that they are responsible to be the Church—reverent, attentive, conscious and aware--prepared before they come.

This awareness of being Church comes from the way people are treated in the liturgy and in the small church community.

> **In the celebration of Mass, the faithful form a holy people, a people of God's own possession and a royal Priesthood, so that they may give thanks to God and offer the unblemished Victim not only by means of the hands of the Priest but also together with him and so they may learn to offer their very selves. They should, moreover, take care to show this by their deep religious sense and their charity toward brothers and**

CONTINUALLY FORMING THE PARISH

sisters who participate with them in the same celebration.
GIRM #95

In our individualistic culture, the communal sense of being Church will not come easily. A network of small church communities can begin to build the parish community in several ways.

1. Parishioners, many for the first time, begin to experience a spiritual bond with other parishioners. They come together in a small church community not as personal friends or from a common interest or project. They come as Catholics preparing for the next Eucharist.
2. The gospel is received communally. The people stay with the gospel and help each other hear it in several different ways.
3. Members share a time of silence to reflect on the gospel with a few life questions.
4. In groups of three or four, parishioners speak and listen to each other.
5. The entire group re-gathers and takes some silence to consider what each will take away when they leave. Some may speak briefly to this point.
6. The extended closing prayer is the response to the Word.

The small church communities are the ground work for a new kind of parish. In the SCC, this simple process repeated week after week prepares parishioners to be a more conscious spiritual community at the Sunday Eucharist.

> From your experience of Sunday liturgy at the parish, how conscious would you say parishioners are of being a holy people offering the Mass together? Try to give some specifics of what you see.
>
> How has your parish community at the Sunday liturgy gone beyond just being friendly?

Chapter Nine
THE PASTOR OF THE PARISH

For I am jealous of you with the jealousy of God since I betrothed you to one husband to present you as a chaste virgin to Christ.
1 Corinthians 11:2

A pastor from "out East" called to ask about keeping their small groups going after the parish had completed a particular Renew program. We explained how the small church communities become the ongoing structure of the parish and how the pastor (and his assistant) would form the leaders of the SCCs. The pastor said "This is more than I wanted."

The pastor calling about continuing small Renew groups obviously cares about the spiritual life of the parish. He already has sought out a program to foster the personal faith of his parishioners and has put some personal time and effort into that program. He has come to see what begins to happen when parishioners are given a way to reflect and hear each other's faith. This pastor took the initiative and called us. He wants to sustain the renewal that has begun but what keeps him, and so many other dedicated priests, from taking the next step? Why can't he get past simply keeping a program going?

We are not claiming to know what motivates every priest in every situation. However, we have worked with pastors and pastoral staffs in every part of North America. Our best "take" on priests is this: To build the parish community from the ground up and to train a whole set of lay pastoral leaders seems overwhelming for pastors trying to manage everything else going on, and especially as more and more pastors are being asked to lead several parishes. One hard-working Detroit pastor simply said, "I can't give this much time." And, most of us pastors are not trained to train others to help us pastor. We would not know where to begin. Many of us would be leading somewhere without knowing from personal experience exactly where we are leading parishioners.

However, there are pastors who have begun and are persevering, slowly forming the parish around the Sunday Eucharist. Two of those priests offer their own reflections on why they are committing to this model for parish, a model that gives them hope and direction.

A long-time pastor, ordained thirty-five years and currently the pastor of the largest parish in the Columbus Diocese:

> *I am Father Charles F. Klinger. I am a priest of the Diocese of Columbus, ordained in 1983. I have been excited about Father Art and Theresa's model of small church communities (SCCs) for almost a quarter of a century in two parishes, including St. Paul the Apostle in Westerville, Ohio, a suburb of Columbus. I have been pastor here for fifteen and a half years and the parish has about four thousand registered families.*
>
> *What attracts me most about this model is the SCCs focus on the upcoming Sunday Gospel which prepares members for the celebration of the Eucharist on the Lord's Day. Every Christian, without exception, has faith to share; and being able to do this in small groups, where each participant can speak in an inviting setting, is deeply enriching spiritually. At the same time, it prepares us to participate more fully in the Eucharist and encourages us to be heralds of the Gospel at home, in the neighborhood, at work, at school, and at play.*
>
> *An essential component of this model is the "Pastoral Facilitators" (PFs) who lead the small church communities. In our parish, a pastoral minister on staff and I carefully discern who have the qualities to be leaders of the SCCs. Through regular meetings of the PFs and an annual retreat, these folks are connected to the pastor of the parish in a close and meaningful way. This link is a truly Catholic element which keeps the PFs in union with the pastor and helps*

them to avoid the temptation of going their own way.

Another extremely important feature of this model is what is often called the "coloring of the parish." This feature entails faith-sharing on the next Sunday's gospel at every meeting that happens in the parish, week in and week out. This enables a sizeable number of parishioners, even those not yet in a small church community, to be part of the process of getting more out of Sunday Mass and thus being better prepared to evangelize. The pastor and his delegate need to be relentless in encouraging and even insisting that this "coloring of the parish" happens at every gathering – regardless of the size or type of meeting.

In our parish school of almost 800 children, faith-sharing happens every week in every grade. In the junior high grades, the teachers focus on the upcoming Gospel. In other grades, the students may do some sharing that arises from posing simple, open-ended questions about their experiences of faith. This process happens in our Parish School of Religion as well. When I can go into the school or PSR classes, I frequently make use of this "coloring." The sharing of the kids is unparalleled in its simplicity and sincerity.

During the time I have been blessed to be pastor here at St. Paul's, we have embarked on some serious brick and mortar projects. Throughout these major building projects, there has also been a deeply meaningful growth in the spiritual lives of our parishioners due to the small church communities and the coloring of the parish. As much as we are proud of our church and school buildings, the building up of the Body of Christ at St. Paul's has been even more impressive.

I am convinced that this building up of the Body of Christ is due in large measure to our deliberate focus on the small church community process.

A young priest starting out:

My name is Father Scott Goodfellow, a priest from the Diocese of Cleveland, Ohio ordained four years ago. I'm writing as a young priest who is still developing his pastoral skills in his second parish assignment. So, I'm not writing this testimony because of my long-term success and implementation of the small church communities in the parish, although I did help implement two initial SCC's at my first parish assignment. I first learned about SCC from Father Bill Thaden and other leaders in the Church using this model. The purpose of this testimony is to reflect, from my perspective as a "millennial" priest, on small communities and their impact on a parish. I hope to make clear that I do see that the small community approach fulfills a deeply needed purpose in the Church: preparing people for Sunday Mass.

I know this sounds simplistic, but the staggering statistics showing the decline of participation at Sunday Mass in many areas of the world indicate a critical pastoral problem in the Church. Preparing people for Sunday Mass so that they know why they are there and what they need from the Lord are indispensable to our restoration of the meaning of Mass among the people of God. The SCC model responds to this grave disconnect by assembling a stable, small group of people, some days before Sunday Mass, to hear the Gospel and ask the right questions: "What questions stir in me as I hear this gospel? What attracts me or challenges me in this gospel?"

This process restores the growth of the Church which Vatican II Constitution on Divine Revelation #8 calls for **"through the contemplation and study made by believers, who treasure these things in their hearts (see Luke 2:19, 51) through a penetrating understanding of the spiritual realities which they experience".** *The goal here is personal appropriation and understanding of how God is gripping me at this time and in this way. Resting with that Word helps one understand the spiritual realities which they experience.*

I am convinced that Eucharist at the Center correctly diagnoses the dilemma and offers the right remedy. Basically, I would describe the dilemma as the disconnect from God that people experience. There are many reasons for this disconnect, but I would point to the underlying cause being a lonely despair that doubts anyone, human or divine, can possibly fill. Modern secularization makes it worse because the secular culture does not believe that spiritual and substantive relationships are even possible. Spiritual life-changing relationships seem to be a fantasy at best

Yet there is hope because of the endurance of the eternal desires of our hearts. The remedy is communion: the restoration of visible, living hope through others, God's Word and Eucharist. The remedy is God always near, that He alone fills that loneliness, and that we are on our way together to the Father's embrace. That Father is faithfully reaching out to us through Christ's Body & Blood and in the Holy Spirit's bond of love. Small church communities bring disciples together under the transformative power of the gospel and prepare them for Eucharistic Communion at Mass.

The Mass is the greatest treasure of the Church for re-establishing communion among God and humanity. The liturgies of the Word and Eucharist at Mass put us personally and communally in touch with God's unique, relentless, salvific love. As a priest, I want to do liturgy well, and that means letting the liturgy be God's work. Yes, good preparation from the ministers is necessary in the hours and days before the liturgy, but all for the sake of allowing God's glory to be experienced at the Mass. I've found that SCC respects God's work in the liturgy precisely by offering small groups of disciples the time to prepare with the gospel, to begin to feel the tremors of the Word in their heart so that they may deeply experience the fruitfulness of the Word and Eucharist at Mass.

One of the SCC facilitators at Ss. Robert & William Parish (where I last served) told me that her small group's time together gives Sunday Mass more meaning and relevance to their lives, encourages them to read scripture, and helps them receive God's blessings of the week with more gratitude. SCC magnifies the graces received at Mass because it makes one's whole life a living liturgy. When a life takes on the character of a living liturgy, the Mass is extended to embrace the entirety of that disciple's existence. This makes him or her a good evangelist. Evangelization, as Pope Francis consistently reminds us in <u>The Joy of the Gospel</u>, is a work of joy.

Sharing the fruits of Christ's victory in one's own life experience is the greatest witness a person can give to the power of the Word and Eucharist alive in them.

As a young priest, I witness a vibrant Catholic Church around me, people who deeply desire the truth, goodness, and beauty of God. But I can also note that we are a Church with some dead weight. We maintain decaying structures that don't necessarily respond to the deepest desires of the human heart for communion. Parish 'activism' often centers around various social events, study groups, or specialized pastoral ministry. When these activities are pursued without a clear connection to Sunday Mass, we lose something of our Catholicity because we bypass or relegate our greatest treasure of the liturgy to being merely 'that one other thing we do over in church.' If our parish 'activities' aren't centered on preparing our people for reception of the Eucharist at Sunday Mass, then we need to reevaluate the purpose of those activities, and be ready to trim the fat in order to focus on the one thing necessary: preparing for communion with God at Mass. This requires a parish plan and vision to always and everywhere place the Eucharist at the center of all our parish activities.

The SCC model takes the Spirit-derived energy of the people of God, directs it with appropriate parish leadership, and allows God to transform His people. The SCCs are a means for people to become fruitful evangelizers who enflesh the gospel and refresh Christ's perennial invitation to be in communion with Him

There is another pastor we have come to know. He has been persevering at this parish plan for the last twelve years. He has learned how to continually form the lay leaders of the small church communities. He sees over time how these leaders have developed but; all this was new for him when he began. This pastor now says, "Where else do you have monthly meetings with top leadership and where else is there such a spiritually transformative experience!" Like so many priests, he had often felt alone in the pastoring task—like it was all up to him. For him, it is no longer so. He likes to quote the *Decree on the Life* and

Ministry of Priest #6:

> **The office of pastor is not confined to the care of the faithful as individuals, but is also properly extended to the formation of a genuine Christian community.**

A parallel teaching, ancient and authentic, comes from the *Catechism of the Catholic Church*.

> **God has, however, willed to make men holy and save them, not as individuals without any bond or link between them, but rather to make them into a people who might acknowledge him and serve him in holiness.** *CCC#781*

How conscious are parishioners coming to Mass that they are being formed into a holy people? That they are intimately linked together by God himself? Is there not some way to make this catechism teaching real and experienced and not only a theory or a concept? The priests quoted earlier and numerous others have found the way. For these particular pastors, the Eucharistic community of Sunday is more attentive, connected and devout because it is knitted together from many more focused smaller communities.

WHERE DOES A PASTOR BEGIN?

We have found that a pastor cannot stick to this plan of building the parish from the ground up without a close collaborator, without someone working with him. There has to be someone the pastor trusts to share this vision. Every pastor we know who has been successful in this model for parish, has such a person. This person working with the pastor we will name the collaborator or the trusted associate.

This collaborator makes two necessary contributions. She or he helps the pastor stay true to the vision of this new kind of parish and helps keep him centered so he does not get lost in all the "urgent" things continually coming at pastors. The trusted associate helps the pastor be a true leader and shepherd. She or he keeps supporting him (and sometimes reminding him) that there is one clear over riding direction: getting parishioners to the Eucharist prepared for transformation.

The second contribution of the collaborator comes much later. It comes as small church communities develop and their leaders need to be selected, formed and deepened. This trusted associate handles much of the work and the details of the work. She or he is available to the leaders of small church communities for consultation and for problem-solving as issues come up. She or he will be involved in planning and facilitating the meetings and retreats for SCC leaders and for providing them with materials. The trusted associate works to make sure the SCC leaders are connecting to the pastor and that the pastor is present at their monthly meetings and retreats, as much as possible. She or he and the pastor together make sure that these lay leaders clearly know they are about a parish structured for the Sunday Eucharist and not simply about running a small group.

The first step for the pastor is to find a trusted associate who will work with him as a collaborator. That person may be on staff or, if need be, a parishioner with vision and organizational skills. The pastor then shares this book chapter by chapter with his collaborator.

In some dioceses, several pastors are cooperating and supporting each other in the parish direction described in this book. Unfortunately, in North America that linkage of parishes moving toward this vision together is not happening very often. In other places (Korea, Philippines, some Latin American and African countries) it happens regularly. Wouldn't that help a pastor if he were meeting with other priests and pastoral workers to reinforce each other and share practical approaches?

Fr. Art

For myself, I have to say I could never have persevered in the parish plan we have described without Theresa Doyle. Theresa was the collaborator for me. We shared this vision and the practice of doing it for twenty years. We kept each other on track. We learned how to do things such as the initial training of lay leaders, the ongoing formation and the annual retreats for them by planning together and evaluating afterwards. We now have a manual available for training of SCC leaders which is included in Volume 2 of this book.

Theresa and Fr. Art

Our book presents a model for parish that offers great hope for the Catholic Church. The Eucharist always is central. These parish structures employ the parishioners themselves as they help each other hear the gospel and prepare for the upcoming Sunday. The role of the pastor as teacher becomes more important than ever because he teaches through the sharing format of the SCC which he and his assistant provide. In this way, he is able to reach many more parishioners than he could reach previously and he is able to extend his teaching office. This parish plan also has the pastor and his assistant forming an entire body of lay leaders assisting them in guiding parishioners through small church communities. And any pastor--no matter what his personal gifts and deficiencies—can do this kind of parish, if he accepts the help of a collaborator.

The next concluding chapter presents two first steps any pastor and his collaborator can take. Those two steps will give them insight into the obstacles already mentioned and how they might go beyond those limitations. More importantly, both steps will give experiences that just reading our book cannot give. Those two experiences will help with the decision whether to go ahead with this structure for parish or not. However it is important to know that persevering in these two steps is essential to see their fruits.

> From the testimonies of priests who are structuring parishes toward the Sunday Eucharist, what encourages you?
>
> What is the main obstacle you have as you consider moving ahead?
>
> If you are a pastor, who might be a possible collaborator with you? Would you consider sharing this book and discussing it with him or her?

Chapter 10
BEGINNINGS

Come to him, a living stone, rejected by human beings but chosen and precious in the sight of God, and, like living stones, let yourselves be built into a spiritual house to be a holy priesthood to offer spiritual sacrifices, acceptable to God through Jesus Christ.
1 Peter 2:4-5

There comes a time to decide—either a decision to put our book on the shelf or to do something different about the parish.

We have tried to make our best case for re-orienting the entire parish toward forming more conscious and spiritually engaged parishioners for Sunday. The goal is simple and clear, but moving the parish in this one direction is a continual process. It involves new parish structures and a new group of lay pastoral leaders.

Suppose you are finding possibilities for your parish in this model. You may well be seeing that the way you have been doing parish is reaching fewer and fewer of its people, especially younger people. From your own familiarity with parish, some of the points presented in this book may be ringing true for you. But, where do you start? As already suggested, the first thing to do is to discuss this book with a trusted collaborator within the parish and, if possible, with pastors/pastoral leaders of other parishes. Then what?

START WITH THE PRIESTS

If the priests are willing to keep working to make this kind of parish happen, it will become the parish direction. After all, it is a total approach to parish. Without the pastor, these proposed structures of small communities and new lay leadership will become only one more program alongside all the other parish programs going on.

We often have found this to be true in working with parishes throughout the U.S. and Canada. The pastor does make the decisive difference on where the parish is going. This is true whether his style is passive or directive, whether he is a quiet man or an outgoing type. The pastor (and the priest assisting him, if there is one) set the parish in its direction. He cannot hand over this directing to another because no one else is the pastor. He can only share the leadership. If the parish leader is not persevering in a specific direction, the flock flounders.

So, why do many parish priests find it difficult to commit personally to this parish plan and persevere in it? For more reasons than we know. But here are some of the reasons priests themselves give are these.

- This is too much with everything else I have to do. One pastor in the Hartford Archdiocese has a good quote on the last six words of a dying priest. "I cannot do one more thing."
- I do not have the confidence that I can do this parish turnaround. I don't have it in me.
- Studies have shown the majority of Catholic priests are introverts. This parish plan seems to need a lot of personal sharing and outreach from the priests.

Because of these and many other reasons, we strongly advise pastors not to begin by making any immediate changes in the parish. Rather, begin with yourself as a pastor or an associate pastor. Just let yourself experience this plan for parish. Your own experience will convince you that this has the potential to revitalize the parish and is worth your determined effort—or not.

We strongly recommend two basic steps that provide the experience needed. These two beginnings may seem simplistic, overly spiritual or naive. We are convinced they are not.

CONTINUALLY FORMING THE PARISH

HEAR THE GOSPEL PERSONALLY

This vision for parish centers on parishioners coming to Mass with the expectation of meeting God. Meeting God means receiving the Scriptures of Sunday as the living Word spoken directly to them. It also means recognizing that Word ultimately as Jesus Christ, the Word made Flesh. That here and now, Christ is leading those who come to want what he wants: communion with himself, and hence, communion with the Church and with the world.

For the priest to have first-hand knowledge of what the people are coming to realize, it seems essential for him to receive the Sunday Scriptures, especially the gospel, in this same way they do. To suggest to Catholic priests that they must hear the gospel first may seem insulting. However, the unrelenting daily responsibilities with so many immediate tasks and self-expectations can absorb pastors. Hearing the gospel and letting the gospel guide them and their work, moment by moment, is not so easy.

Fr. Art

Much of my ministry as a priest has been doing the work of Christ. I have been less aware of what Jesus Christ was doing in each situation and then cooperating and co-working with him. The starting point was my doing. What I would like to develop is my getting attuned to what he is doing. Then, join in.

I always spent time with the upcoming Sunday gospel. On occasion, I met with other priests, deacons and interested laypeople to prepare the homily. The point is that it was to prepare the homily. I was looking to extract the best meaning so there could be a good message to the people at Mass. It has taken me a long time to begin to hear the upcoming gospel as spoken to me personally, as a living word by a God interested in me.

I would have said, "Who has time for all this!" But now I have found a practice that helps me listen better. It is to spend time each day with the upcoming gospel of Sunday—even forty-five to sixty minutes when I am disciplined enough to make the time. I do not go to commentaries or do exegesis for the first days. I simply hear or read the gospel over and over, staying with a single word or phrase, asking God to show me, and then I respond in some way. The questions posted on our web-site often focus my wandering mind which consistently goes to what I must do or have left undone. From receiving the gospel in this way, I am becoming more conscious that Christ is creating his Church and me with and in the Church. I am more awake to what he is doing in the upcoming Eucharist.

Theresa and Fr. Art

We are seeing priests pulled in many directions. There are fewer of them having to do more. Many are responsible for several merged or clustered parishes. Some dioceses have raised the retirement age. It is no wonder that a pastor or soon to be pastor would balk at a parish plan which, at first, seems to involve more work.

That is why we ask priests to begin with the Gospel. It is there that they can realize who really is leading the parish and where he wants to take the parish. Through the Gospel heard again and again, Jesus Christ is given a better chance of becoming the director. And gradually, a different mind-set takes hold of his priest.

To us, it seems the main task of pastors and pastoral leaders is to pay attention to the movements of God. In other words simply paying attention to what God is doing. The starting point is for the leader to recognize how God is prompting and moving in their own life first, then in people's lives and in the community of faith.

> **Catechesis aims at putting "people . . . in communion . . . with Jesus Christ: only he can lead us to the love of the Father in the Spirit and make us share in the life of the Holy Trinity."**
> *CCC #426*

Is not the Church teaching that the shepherd also must be a sheep, the teacher must first be a learner? The Gospel forming the Church is the same Gospel forming the leader of that Church.

CONTINUALLY FORMING THE PARISH
HEARING THE GOSPEL IN A COMMUNAL SETTING

We believe that there is one more experience for a priest before he decides on any action for the parish. It would be most helpful for the pastor and his collaborator to hear the gospel in a communal setting, in a small group of about eight or nine parishioners. Preferably the two of them would be in different groups. All the instructions that follow for the priest would also be true for the collaborator. However each of them being in a newly formed but different group would give each their own unique experience. This would be helpful as they determined the future direction of the parish.

From the many places where we have worked and from conversations we have had with pastoral people of several continents, we have come to one conclusion. The best hope for the priest to make an informed judgment about the structure of small church communities for the parish is for him to enter into one of these for a good while. How else can a pastoral leader come in contact with everyday parishioners sharing the Sunday gospel! How can he come to see for himself the gradual effect they have on each other's faith! By being part of this beginning group, a priest can have first-hand knowledge of laypeople helping each other prepare to hear God's word at Mass. Of course, the small group experience takes some time of meeting regularly. We recommend staying with the group for the better part of a year.

After a year of a small community, a pastor and his collaborator would know experientially what the small church community is. The pastor would gain confidence that with the help of a strong collaborator, he is capable of this parish plan. Then comes the judgment for the parish.

> Can this simple gathering of very ordinary parishioners receiving the gospel together and hearing each other connect their lives to that gospel be the parish's mustard seed for growth?
>
> Can this simple gathering, if it is replicated in an ever-increasing

number of groups, change the Sunday crowd?

Can the Word of God that calls the Church into existence at the Eucharist be heard with more attention and received with more depth because of such small church communities?

Finally, is this the best way for the parish to go?

Again, this is taking the time of the pastor, time which he thinks he does not have to give. However the priest is considering a major course for the parish, a steady path for the years ahead. He is deciding as well about new ways he will operate as a priest and what his priorities will become. Personally experiencing a small church community gives the priest a very good basis for whatever decision he will make.

What does appeal to many priests and pastoral leaders about this model for parish is that it allows Christ to lead. There is an attraction because their leadership has a clear focus—bringing parishioners into direct contact with Christ, with his very Word, with his desires and his actions. Many documents on the priesthood converge to support the way such priests have come to see this as their task. Here is one.

> **It is in representing him (Christ) that the bishop or priest acting in the person of Christ the head (in persona Christi capitis) presides over the assembly, speaks after the readings, receives the offerings, and says the Eucharistic Prayer.**
> *CCC #1348*

The priest re-presents Christ, that is makes him present. It is not as if Jesus Christ is somewhere else watching the various parts of the Mass as they happen, quite content that his priest is doing all this for him.

The same CCC #1348 makes sure to say this.

> **At the head of the Eucharistic assembly is Christ himself, the principal agent of the Eucharist.**

The principal agent is the one making something happen. Only Jesus Christ can bring about deep and lasting change in people. People's readiness has a lot to do with how deep and lasting that change can be. Priests lead best when they let Christ lead and that includes when they help parishioners come better prepared for the action of Christ. As the Scripture quote at the beginning of this chapter says, "Come to him, a living stone. And, like living stones, let yourselves be built into a spiritual house."

Coming to Jesus Christ, that "living stone," is why the small church community exists. It is a way to let him build that spiritual house, the Church. The SCC can be like a practice for the large Church Community at the Sunday Eucharist. In the small group experience, parishioners get the sense of Christ uniting them, speaking to them, and waiting for a response. These parishioners then come to Mass looking for the fullness of the Lord's actions to take place there. They come with greater readiness and expectation.

The pastor of the parish will choose small church communities as his plan for the parish or he will choose some other way. Whatever path he chooses, there is one question to be addressed: What is the most effective way that helps the parish to come to the Eucharist prepared to engage the "principal agent" who is Christ?

THE PRIEST'S EXPERIENCE OF A BEGINNING GROUP

In this beginning group of which he is a part, the pastor (or the parish leader) may or may not learn anything new from parishioners. That is not the goal here. The purpose is for the priest to notice the movements of God in the people and in himself.

It is important for the pastor to know the elements of a small church community. If he chooses the parish model in this book, it would be helpful for him to know, from experience, some of the inner life of these small communities. If he chooses to go another way, he has at least become familiar with how regular laypeople can have a tremendous influence on the faith of the parish.

So, we advise creating one small beginning group and simply being part of it but not leading the group. In choosing the members for this small group, the pastor might want to look for some people who have the qualities to possibly lead new groups in the future. But, it is not advisable to speak of that yet since this determination will be made only later on. At this point, they do not even know what a small church community is. He asks them to accept only what they can accept now—to be part of a beginning group with him.

This beginning group with the pastor will disband eventually. Should the pastor and his collaborator take the next steps of forming other beginning small church communities; the pastor's role will be to give his time to the leaders of the newly forming groups. These SCC leaders will form a group around the pastor and his collaborator and will become his continuing small group. This leadership formation is described in Volume 2. But for now, this inaugural small gathering would simply experience the format of a small church community around the upcoming gospel.

To be a part of a small group receiving the Sunday gospel, the pastor will have to resist being the answer man and teacher of the group. Right at the start, he will have to tell the others that he simply wants to be a part of the group and to experience what they will experience. The priest's purpose now is to be a member and to simply experience receiving the gospel in a small group setting. The step-by-step process for a small community to begin and grow is clearly laid out in Appendix 1 at the end of this book. As mentioned earlier the material for each week is found at www.naprc.net. The one running the group simply has to follow the format and agenda and keep to the time allotted for each part of the ninety minute meeting. Starting a meeting and ending a meeting on time is very important. So the pastor will need to find the person able to stay to an agenda and at the same time make people feel comfortable. He or his collaborator will have to prepare the person leading the small group to make sure they are comfortable leading and clearly understands the meeting format.

For the priest, being a member of the beginning group is not easy. Parishioners naturally defer to him, looking for approval or disapproval. Some will address theological questions to him and he will have to explain that this is not the place for those questions. Depending on his personality, the priest may have to resist correcting someone's misperceptions or giving pastoral counseling for a problem stated in the group. It may be difficult for him to share from his own experience and to speak of personal uncertainty—just as it is difficult for laypeople, especially men, to speak of these things. Listening, really listening can be his greatest challenge. But, if the priest is to experience the small community format and the transforming effects of hearing the gospel in a communal setting, he will have to enter into the experience.

MEMBERS FOR THE BEGINNING GROUP

The beginning group should be composed of everyday parishioners. The group should be a mix of people for whom this experience is new. Most importantly, they must be willing to give the time it takes for the group to develop and deepen. They also must be personally open to the experience. Parishioners already having a particular familiarity with other kinds of faith sharing groups may bring too much of their experience to this group. They can dominate or overwhelm without meaning to do so.

The beginning group should resemble the parish. It is not meant to be a common interest group. There should be diversity. It surely should include younger married people, a single person beginning a career or a college student if possible. For starters it would be best not to include the very devout people often present at every parish event and devotion. They can be included in future groups. It is best if the beginning members of this group are not personal friends. And, men simply must be at least half of the members. Ten is a good number. A home setting is ideal but a comfortable room at the parish site could work.

The people will say yes because the pastor or significant staff member personally asks each of them. They will try something that is new and unpredictable because of a certain trust in the person asking.

At the first meeting of this beginning group, the pastor welcomes and thanks people for saying yes to an unknown. He explains the purpose of the group: something new for the parish, being done at parishes in many places and his own need to experience it for himself so he can pursue or not pursue forming these small groups in the parish. He speaks about his role in the small group as a member and not the leader so he can just experience the group and the process of hearing the Gospel along with everyone in the group.

The pastor then introduces the person who will lead the meetings, explaining that he or she is organized and will simply lead us through the format for the meetings. After being introduced the leader will take over using the appropriate agenda.

> How much time do you personally spend with the upcoming gospel?
>
> Do you find that your time with the gospel is primarily for homily preparation or planning a lesson?
>
> Have you shared in the past or do you presently share the Sunday gospel with others in a group setting? If so, what was positive and not positive with the experience? What would make it better?

CONCLUSION

There is need of only one thing.
Luke 10:42

Along with many others working in parishes and dioceses, we think this plan for parish finds its support in the Church herself.

> **The other sacraments, and indeed all ecclesiastical ministries and works of the apostolate, are bound up with the Eucharist and are oriented toward it.** *CCC #1324 referring to the Constitution on the Church 11*

Some priests will not choose this kind of total approach toward the Eucharist. They may be waiting for something better to come along, something more to their liking. However, there is nothing better than the Eucharist! The one thing that limits the power of Jesus Christ in the action of the Mass is how willing people are to let him form them and lead them. It takes both parties for communion. This entire parish plan is about parishioners helping each other to let Christ lead. Both people and priests are about coming to the Eucharist more docile to the Lord.

After all is said and done:

> **The sacraments are efficacious because in them Christ himself is at work: it is he who baptizes, he who acts in his sacraments in order to communicate the grace that each sacrament signifies.** *CCC #1127*

How many Catholics would say "Jesus Christ baptized me"? How many priest presiders spontaneously say that Christ is the principal actor making everything happen in the Mass? Christ is the one gathering these people. He is speaking these scriptures. He is the one offering his life to the Father and asking all of us to join him with the offering of our own personal lives. He is the only one who can bring about life-changing communion. Really, this is his Mass.

TWO SERIOUS RESERVATIONS

One reservation comes from some priests who have asked us if these small church communities preparing for Mass are the only thing going on in the parish. After all, there seems to be such a strong emphasis for them.

Our response is that some parish programs may be downsized or eliminated so parishioners can focus their time commitment on what has the greatest potential to transform the parish. Other parish activities may need to continue but everything is oriented toward the Sunday Eucharist and prepares parishioners for Sunday. And, priority attention and time is given to forming lay pastoral leaders for small church communities.

Another reservation comes from some who say SCCs are not for everyone. They would say there are many spiritual paths.

True enough. But the Word of God is for everyone. The Eucharist is for everyone. Preparing for the Eucharist is for everyone. The parish is for everyone. Each person brings her or his own life experiences to the liturgy and likewise to the small church community. In fact, like the Mass, the SCC is the place where the many paths of spirituality can come together, as we prepare for the upcoming Sunday Eucharist.

A TIME TO DECIDE

What is an overworked and overextended pastor to do? He may as well put his time and energy into what will make the greatest difference for the Church. That pastor will have to move from the mindset of what he has to get done and change the focus to what Christ is doing.

The Mass is the experience where most Catholics do come to encounter Christ. If people—young and old—are to understand what being Catholic means, the Eucharist teaches it best. The Church herself says this very thing.

Today, many are not staying with the Church. The Sunday celebration done well at least gives them the best possible experience of Church. They should know what they are leaving or for what they stay.

As the Church today faces so many signs of loss, is it not time to step away from our discouragement and depend on Christ to form his Church in the particular way he has given? Let him do what we cannot! Our pastoral work is to bring the parish fully present and available to him so he can do his work.

A pastor cannot do everything. But, at the end of the day or at retirement, hopefully he has stayed with a clear and worthy direction for the parish.

If you have read this book and are given hope by this vision and want further information or have questions go to National Alliance of Parishes Restructuring into Communities at: www.naprc.net

NAPRC (National Alliance of Parishes Restructuring into Communities) is a nonprofit national organization formed to help pastors and parish leaders. Our purpose is to focus the parish on the Sunday Eucharist and ordinary parishioners regularly helping each other prepare for that Eucharist. We are within the Roman Catholic Archdiocese of Detroit.

APPENDIX 1

MEETINGS FOR INITIATING AND FORMING A NEW SMALL CHURCH COMMUNITY (SCC)

General information to ensure the success of a new SCC

It is important that a new group meet for *eight consecutive weeks* so that a bond can start to develop. The eighth week would be the time for this new group to evaluate how things are going and to determine if they will continue to meet weekly or if meeting every other week would work best for them.

The agenda should never exceed ninety minutes. The leader should pay strict attention to time and adapt the agenda accordingly. A short social time with simple refreshments should take place once the meeting is over. The social time is important and offers a great opportunity for further bonding within the group. Placing it after the meeting, allows for those who have to leave immediately, for another commitment, to do so.

Progression For A New Group Being Formed

- Meetings 1, 2, and 3 will be abbreviated from what will eventually be the regular ongoing format for the meetings. This is done to allow time for introductions and for the group just to get to know each other and become comfortable. These agendas are clearly laid out in the pages that follow.

- For the 4th meeting and the following meetings, the "getting to know you" time is dropped. The meetings will now include an extended closing prayer time. Allowing sufficient time for the closing prayer is very important. It is a time for people to once again be aware of what God has been saying throughout the meeting and respond to God.

- The 8th meeting allows time for the group to evaluate how things have been going and to make some decisions about how they will proceed. The group may decide to continue weekly (which is the ideal) or perhaps find that meeting every other week works better for all members. This meeting will also be a time of recommitment to the group.

- Eventually, after the 8th week and when the group is ready, Journaling and Prayer Partners will be introduced.

Essentials to Forming a New Group to Become a Fruitful SCC

- It is ideal to have two trained leaders for each group. The leader or leaders will facilitate all the meetings. In most cases these co-leaders find it best to take turns facilitating the meetings by alternating weeks.

- The environment must be physically comfortable, and people must feel free to talk.

- The group should be told and occasionally reminded that what is said in the group is meant to stay in the group.

- Stay true to the agenda: Always do one-on-one. Always break into small groups of 3 or 4. Always give quiet time before large group feedback. Begin on time and end on time.

- Members should take turns hosting if possible. However if meetings are best held at the same location all the time, members of the group should take turns bringing simple refreshments.

- Members must make attendance a priority. Exceptions, of course, do present themselves, i.e., sickness, overtime work, etc. Missing a meeting should be the exception and not the norm.

People attending meetings only when they feel like it seriously hinders the SCC from growing and deepening.

- Once the group is formed, there is not an open invitation to visitors or new members. Occasionally there may be a need for groups to merge to form a new group or bring in a new member or two if the group size has dwindled due to members moving away or passing away. It is important to know that adding even one new member significantly changes the group. Therefore there is an appropriate way for it to happen. This process can be found in the Pastoral Facilitator training manual in Volume 2 of *Eucharist at the Center*

- In the event the SCC chooses to take a summer break due to vacations, the date the group will reconvene should always be established before the start of the break. A break from the weekly or bi-monthly meeting is a good time to work in a family social, such as a barbeque or picnic, as a way to keep the group connected.

AGENDA FOR 1ST MEETIING

Welcome and Overview of Meeting – (5 mins.)
(It is helpful to use Name tags for the first few meetings.)

- Leader/leaders welcome everyone, introduce themselves, and say that they have been asked to lead the meetings for this group. Let everyone know that they are first and foremost members of the group, but since someone has to lead the meetings, they agreed to do it.

- Leader explains that at these meetings we will be spending time with the gospel for the upcoming Sunday. Listening is what is most important in this group. Everyone participates by listening and then by contributing their thoughts and insights when they can. Listening is essential for this group to work. We are meant to listen for understanding and not necessarily for agreement. Respect for each other is key. The way you see things may not be the way I or others see things. We don't have to convince anyone of anything. We just need to listen to each other respectfully. In the process of our time together, it is God who changes people's hearts and minds. We simply help each other to pay attention.

- It is also important to know that what is said in this group is meant to stay with this group.

- We are asked to make a commitment to attend these meetings for eight consecutive weeks. What is necessary for this group to work and bear fruit is that everybody makes this a priority and comes each week. Being here is very important. Meeting weekly for the first eight sessions will enable us to get to know each other and build trust. After the eighth week, together we will evaluate our group and decide how we will proceed. We may want to continue to meet weekly or decide every other week works best for us.

- The meetings will be ninety minutes. We will have simple refreshments at the end of each meeting. If there is anyone who cannot stay after the ninety minute meeting time that is okay. For today/tonight, I brought some refreshments, but this is something we can take turns doing. Refreshments are meant to be very simple.

Large group - Introductions (10 – 15 mins.)

- Say; "We are going to start today by taking some time to get to know each other a little bit."
- Ask everyone to say their name, married or not, children or not, grandchildren? Do they work? Are they a stay-at-home mom or dad, a student or retired? How long have they have been a parishioner of _____? Why did they say yes to be part of this group? Repeat questions a second time!
- After introductions - One on one (5-8 mins.)
- Turn to the person next to you. Each person responds to the following questions.
- Over the last week or the last few days, when or where in your life have you been most aware of God?
- Over the last week or the last few days what has been most challenging to you? Or what has taken energy from you?
- Repeat questions a second time!

Hearing the Word of God

- Find three people ahead of time to do Bible enthronement as explained below in # 1.

- Also, find someone who will proclaim the gospel as explained below in # 2.

Explain to the group the process that will be used to hear the gospel. Say: "We are going to hear the gospel for this coming Sunday proclaimed two times. The first time we will just hear it. Then there will be a pause. The second time we hear it, pay attention to a word or phrase that strikes you. After we have completely heard the gospel the second time, we will each just say the word or phrase that came to our mind, without any other comment or explanation. These words will be said in no particular order. Just simply say the word or phrase that came to you. It is okay to repeat what someone else has said."

1. Leader; pray aloud in your own words asking the Holy Spirit to open the minds and hearts of all who are gathered, to hear God's Word.

   Bible Enthronement - Play the opening song, while three people carry in a lit candle, the Bible, and a crucifix and place them on a center table. – (5 mins.)

2. After Bible Enthronement, hear the gospel proclaimed two times as previously explained. – (4-5 mins.)

3. Quiet time alone with the gospel – Give a handout with just the words of the gospel.
   Allow some quiet time for everyone to read it. – (2 mins.)

4. Alone time continues - After people have had time to read the gospel, say: "Take a few moments of quiet to pay attention to what attracts you or gets your attention in this gospel. There will be a time to talk about this question later but for now just quietly notice what attracts you in this gospel." *Pause for a few moments.*

   Then say: "Take a few more moments of quiet to notice, Does anything in this gospel cause resistance in you? Or does it challenge you in some way?" *Pause for about 30 seconds.*

EUCHARIST AT THE CENTER

5. Hand out the short commentary and life faith questions on the gospel only after the alone time with the gospel itself. Allow quiet time for people to read and reflect on the commentary and questions before getting into a small group. (2 - 3 mins.)

6. Small group of three people – (10 mins)
   Instruct the group that the idea in not to answer all of the questions they have been given but each person should speak to one or two questions that connect for them.
   Also, this is not the time to give advice or try to help someone figure things out. It is time to just hear each other.

7. Large group quiet/reflection time – (2 mins.)
   Say: "Take a few minutes of quiet and consider the questions; What are you hearing for yourself or becoming aware of today as you hear this gospel and have spent time talking with each other?"

8. Large group response – (5 - 10 mins.)
   Say: "Would anyone be willing to say what you are hearing or something you have become aware of throughout our time of listening to the gospel and talking with each other?"

9. Personal reflection – (2 mins.)
   Say: "Take another few minutes of quiet to consider your life in the days or weeks ahead of you. What difference can the gospel we received here today make in your life? **pause** How will those you encounter today, tomorrow, or any time this week be affected by the gospel you have heard today? **pause**. Pay attention if anyone, in particular, comes to mind for you." After quiet time, say, "The answers to these questions do not always come to us immediately. These are questions we might need to stay with and in fact, ask ourselves throughout the week ahead."

10. Closing Prayer – Use simple closing prayer for the first three weeks. – (10 mins.)
    For example - Ask; "Would anyone like us to pray for anything in particular?" Our response to our prayers will be "Lord hear our prayer." After prayers of petition, the Leader follows by

praying a simple prayer in your own words then say: "Together let us pray the prayer Jesus taught us, Our Father . . ."

Announcements – (2 mins.)
Remind the group that we are asked to make these meetings a priority in order to give them a chance to become a meaningful experience for all of us. People coming only occasionally do not allow for this to happen.

We are asked to commit to eight consecutive weeks. At the eighth meeting, we will do an evaluation together to determine the future of this group.

Have people write their names, phone numbers, and emails on a list for the leaders to have.   Copies of this can be handed out to the group in the next couple of weeks if everyone is comfortable with that.

Encourage group members to read the daily Scriptures of the Church. It is also very helpful to read the upcoming Sunday readings especially the gospel before coming to our weekly meetings. This is the best way to prepare for our time together. The daily readings of the Church can be found on line at the United States Conference of Catholic Bishops website (uscccb.org).

Other announcements: Where will we meet next? Who will bring simple refreshments?

MEETINGS 2 AND 3 - DO NOT EXCEED 90 MINS.

To help the group continue to get to know each other better, start with a simple ice breaker question. Take one of the following examples or something similar. Introduce the ice breaker as something we will do for a few weeks simply to help us get to know each other.

- Where is one place you have visited that you would definitely return to if given a chance? Why would you want to go back?
- Talk about your favorite pastime when you were a child and

why you enjoyed it so much. What's a favorite pastime you have now?

- If you could have dinner with anyone in the world, who would that be and why?

After the ice breaker, move into the agenda as laid out in meeting one. Remember the small group time with the gospel commentary and questions should only be about ten minutes, to allow for time spent with the icebreaker question.

Use a simple closing prayer to end the meeting.

MEETING 4, 5, 6, 7 – DO NOT EXCEED 90 MINS.

Begin by letting people settle in with casual conversation. Then go directly to the one-on-one. "Where I've been most aware of God this week? Where I've been challenged this week?"

Use the agenda laid out in meeting one. However, the small group time with the gospel commentary and questions can increase to 15 – 20 minutes.

The "Extended Closing Prayer" (which is available to you along with the weekly gospel, commentary, and questions) is used from now on. It will take 15 – 20 minutes.

MEETING 8

This is the time for the group to do an evaluation of how things are going. Follow the same agenda you have been using to hear the Sunday gospel. However, to keep the meeting to ninety minutes and yet allow enough time for the group evaluation, the time spent in a small group discussion with the questions on the gospel will need to be shortened. Additionally, the large group feedback time should be shortened to just a few comments. Use the closing prayer that follows the evaluation part of this meeting.

After having heard the gospel, the small group discussion, and large group feedback use the following process for the group evaluation.- (60 mins.)

Group Affirmation- (10 mins.)
Hand out an index card and a pen to each person. Have them write their name on the card.

Instruct the group to pass their card to the person on their right. On the card they have received, they are to write down what they are grateful for in that person or what gift they recognize in that person. After writing they will pass the card they have to the next person on the right. The cards will continue to be passed around the group until everyone has received their own card back. Play soft instrumental music while this is happening.

Once each card has gone around the circle, and everyone has received his or her own card back, allow time for people to read their card. Let the music continue for this. (3 mins.)

After people have had a chance to read their cards of affirmation, say: "Many gifts have been shared throughout our time together over the last eight weeks. We are going to take time now to talk about what these meetings have been like for us."

Alone time with the following three questions.- (5 mins.)
Hand out a sheet of paper with these questions.

- How would you compare this group today to this group eight weeks ago?
- What positive things have happened for you personally because of meeting with this group?
- As we move ahead, what are the challenges that will make your committing to this group difficult?

Large group – (20 mins.)
Take one question at a time and go around the circle, giving everyone a chance to speak.

EUCHARIST AT THE CENTER

Recommitment – (10 mins.)

Say: "This group is meant to have experienced the beginnings of a small church community. To be a small church community, it is important that we meet regularly to help each other live more fully as the church. We come together to help each other prepare to hear and receive God's Word which he speaks to the whole Church each Sunday. This prepares us to experience the Eucharist more fully and be able to better live our lives every day as a disciple of Christ. This group can change each one of us if we let it. It can and will help us to be more aware of Christ living in us and enabling us to live as His disciple. For that to happen, it takes a commitment to the group. Coming occasionally would hurt the group. There are of course some understandable reasons why someone may not be able to make a meeting, such as sickness or work. In those situations just let us know.

It is ideal for a small church community to meet every week to help each other prepare to experience the upcoming Sunday Eucharist. Is this a possibility for us? Would you be willing and able to commit to meeting every week as we have been doing? Or is every other week more realistic for us?"

After discussion of the proposed questions and it has been identified who will commit to continuing, determine where you will meet and who will bring refreshments.

Closing Prayer– (10 mins.)
Play - "We Have Been Told" by David Haas

All stand - Say: "What are you grateful for from out time together today? In a few words let's each say something we are grateful for from our time together or perhaps say something you are grateful for about this group."

After everyone has spoken, the Leader says: "Let us pray for each other that we will continue to grow and deepen as God's church, and as well we pray for our whole parish. Our Father..."

Note to leader – From now on Appendix 2 – Agenda for Maturing and Mature SCCs will be used for meetings.

APPENDIX 2

MATURING AND MATURED SMALL CHURCH COMMUNITIES AGENDA

Meeting designed for 90 min.

Welcome and Greetings – (3 mins.)

Prayer Partners – (8 - 10 minutes)
Replacing the one-on-one as done in the past, members of the group will pair off as prayer partners. They will continue to meet as prayer partners at each meeting, for an extended period, usually for about 6 months. Then prayer partners can be reassigned. Questions for the prayer partners to use are found in Appendix 3. *(An option - For convenience, Appendix 3 is set up to create a prayer card that can fit into a wallet.)*

Hear the Word – total time for #1 - #11, (approximately 55 mins.)
Use the gospel for the upcoming Sunday. Ideally, the gospel should be proclaimed from the enthroned Bible that is in the same translation as the one used for Sunday liturgy.

Proclamation of the Word
We hear the Word proclaimed–simply hear it and receive it.

1. Before hearing the gospel, **the leader explains to the group** that the gospel will be heard two times. The first time the gospel is proclaimed just hear it. The second time it is proclaimed, pay attention to any word or phrase that gets your attention or strikes you in some way. After the second reading is complete, each of us will say out loud the word or phrase that got our attention. Simply say the word or phrase without explanation or

comment. And it is okay if you repeat what someone else has said. We won't go in any specific order for this. Just say the word or phrase when you are ready.

2. Opening prayer – The leader prays in his or her own words asking the Holy Spirit to open the minds and hearts of all gathered to receive God's Word.
3. Bible enthronement takes place while the opening song is played.
4. First proclamation of the gospel by a member of the group who is prepared to do so.

Everyone listen.

5. Pause for a time of silence about twenty seconds.
6. Second proclamation of the gospel.

Each person speaks a word or phrase that has stood out for them.

Options - In place of *Lectio Divina* (repeating a word or phrase that strikes you), on occasion after hearing the gospel a second time, have group pair off and retell the gospel in his or her own words to each other. Or a second option is to instruct members that as they hear the gospel the second time, to simply put themselves in t he gospel and become one of the people there. Then after the second proclamation, turn to one other person and each talk about what that experience was like.

7. Quiet time alone with the gospel – (2 or 3 mins.)
   Hand out just a copy of the gospel. Instruct people to take a few minutes of quiet to read the gospel and just stay with the words.
8. Alone time continues. After people have taken time to read the gospel, say: "Without comment, quietly become aware of what attracts you or gets your attention in this gospel." Pause for about one minute. Then say: "Without comment, quietly become aware of what challenges you or in some way causes you to feel resistance."
9. Small groups of three to four faith-sharing. (15-20 mins.)
   Hand out a short commentary and life faith questions. Com-

mentary should be factual and true to the gospel. The two alone time questions should be included along with three or four simple life-faith questions relevant to the gospel.

Allow some alone time of quiet with the handout before getting into a small group. Remind everyone that the idea is not to answer every question but to respond to one or two that speak particularly to them.

10. Large group quiet reflection – (3 or 4 mins.)
    On returning to the large group, give people some alone time to write in their journals their response to the following questions: What are you hearing in this gospel today? Or What are you becoming more aware of through hearing God's Word and spending time talking with each other?

11. Large group reactions. (10 mins)
    Say: "Would anyone be willing to say what you are hearing God say today? Or What are you becoming more aware of as a result of hearing God's Word and spending time talking with each other? Do not say what others shared in your small group. Speak only of what you are personally hearing or becoming aware of."

12. Alone time reflection / personal application- (1 - 2 mins.)
    Say: "Take a few minutes of quiet to consider, having received the gospel today, how will it impact your life in the week or weeks ahead of you? How might it impact those you will meet this week? **pause** Is there someone in particular, you might share the Good News with?" Repeat questions.
    After quiet time, say: "The answers to these questions do not always come to us immediately. These are questions we might need to stay with and in fact ask ourselves throughout the week ahead."

We Respond to God – Closing Prayer (20 mins.)

Use the extended closing prayer that is part of the weekly meeting material prepared for SCCs available online at www.naprc.net

Announcements – (5 minutes)
Who will host the next meeting? Who will bring refreshments?

Refreshments – keep it simple!

APPENDIX 3

If creating appendix 3 into a Prayer Card for prayer partners, it can be formatted to the size of a business card, in order to fit into a wallet.

Front of card

> Prayer is the art of hearing and responding to God revealing himself to us moment by moment.

Back of card

> The last time we met you asked me to pray for _____. How are things going? How is daily prayer going for you? Are you able to make time to pray? What are you becoming aware of in prayer? Since we last met when have you been most aware of God? What do you personally need me to pray for?

www.ingramcontent.com/pod-product-compliance
Ingram Content Group UK Ltd.
Pitfield, Milton Keynes, MK11 3LW, UK
UKHW022224230426
12048UKWH00016BA/1044